This book is a work of non-fiction intended for self-help, educational and professional purposes. The views, opinions, and interpretations expressed herein are solely those of the author. While every effort has been made to ensure accuracy and reliability, the author and publisher disclaim any liability or responsibility for any actions taken or not taken based on the content of this book.

For permissions, inquiries, or requests for bulk or institutional orders, please contact: info@cognicare.co.za

First edition: August 2025

ISBN: 978-183492-950-7

Contents

Prologue: A Vision for Culturally Integrated Counselling

I have never felt a more unrelenting need for an all-inclusive, approach to counselling than in our world today, which is both amazingly diverse and ever more interconnected. I recognize that people bring their own distinct cultural identities, beliefs, and methods of healing into the counselling space. As a counsellor, I see it as my responsibility to understand the full person, their cultural background, perspective, and life story—rather than merely just rushing into the counselling relationship.

In my work, I have come to appreciate the unique contributions of Chinese therapeutic models, South African healing methods, and Western psychology. Each of these traditions offer important insights into pain, human nature, and recovery, while also carrying its own cultural assumptions and limitations. By integrating them, I aim not only to broaden the scope and depth of my counselling practice but also to expand my understanding of what it truly means to provide effective, culturally attuned care.

Through this book, I hope to provide fellow counsellors with a roadmap for navigating the challenges of cultural diversity in their practice. I draw on the knowledge of these various systems to highlight both the difficulties and the tremendous benefits of incorporating multiple cultural models into counselling. Beyond theory, I share practical tools, case studies, and strategies that I have found useful in adapting approaches to deliver culturally competent care that genuinely resonates with clients from all walks of life.

I believe that integrated counselling will be essential to promoting mental and emotional well-being for everyone, regardless of cultural background, as our global community continues to evolve. My aim is not only to support healing on an individual level but also to honor and acknowledge the cultures and traditions that have shaped each client, recognizing that these cultural contexts are central to the journey of recovery.

ACKNOWLEDGMENTS

First and foremost, I would like to acknowledge God for opening this door and guiding me through this massive journey. Without His grace, wisdom, and direction, this journey I am on would not have begun, this is only the beginning.

I would also like to express my deepest gratitude to my husband, whose unwavering support has allowed me to focus on my personal development while he tirelessly looks out for us. Your belief in me and your commitment to our family have been a source of strength and motivation throughout this journey and you continue to encourage me, always painting out the bigger picture for me.

I am profoundly grateful to Tina, who I recognize as a divine connection from God. Your faith, guidance, and willingness to listen to the Lord's direction have been invaluable, and I am thankful for the ways in which you have supported me to take this path. I'd also like to acknowledge Queena for being a vessel.

I would like to acknowledge my former boss, Dr. Kaggwa. When we first met, he shared with me that he believed I was a mental health practitioner at heart, and that working in a research institute was part of my journey to where I was meant to go. At the time, I only partially saw the picture but now I see the vision clearly and recognize the lessons I was meant to learn along the way. Thank you for your wisdom, guidance, and belief in my path. On this note I would also like to acknowledge my friend Daphney who was also a vessel.

Lastly, I acknowledge my sweet Eden who has also been my co-pilot. Thank you for taking your naps when I most needed you to.

To my mom Georgina.

Chapter 1

Comprehending Cultural Background in Psychological Counselling

1.1 The Role of Culture in influencing Psychological Well-being

One thing I've learned is that culture serves as the basis for all counselling interactions, influencing the client's worldview, emotional expression, distress perception, and understanding of the healing process. Based on my experience, cultural circumstances affect how psychological symptoms are expressed, what is considered "normal" or "pathological," and what coping mechanisms are useful or acceptable in society. In certain cultures, for instance, emotional difficulties may manifest mainly as physical symptoms, but in others, social or spiritual interventions are essential for relieving anguish. To appropriately assess and address a client's requirements, counsellors must be aware of these nuances.

As a counsellor, getting a thorough understanding of these cultural factors is the first step I take towards offering skilled and sympathetic counselling. Additionally, as counsellors we need to develop reflective awareness, cultural literacy, and sensitivity to the social, family, and spiritual frameworks of our clients. This would work by identifying both obvious and hidden sides of culture, ranging from language and traditions to values, worldviews, and interpersonal standards. We as counsellors can adopt an atmosphere of trust and cooperation by recognizing and honoring the client's cultural perspective, guaranteeing that interventions are relevant, moral, and significant. Finally, by meeting clients where they are, we can agree that culturally sensitive counseling improves counselling relationships and promotes more lasting and successful results.

Cultural Relativism

I believe that the idea that cultural beliefs and practices must be understood in their own context, rather than judged through the lens of another culture, is at the heart of culturally sensitive counselling. This principle acknowledges that mental health is not a universal construct, but rather one that is deeply shaped by social norms, values, traditions and worldviews. I learned this from a cross-cultural psychology text. For example, in many Western contexts, openly discussing personal struggles may be seen as a sign of strength and self-awareness, while in some African or Asian communities, such openness might be viewed as inappropriate or even shameful, with preference given to communal support or spiritual rituals instead. I've seen both cases in my community. Neither approach is inherently right or wrong—they simply reflect different cultural frameworks for coping and healing.

In cross-cultural counselling, this understanding is critical because what is considered "normal" or "healthy" in one culture may be interpreted very differently in another. Practices such as ancestor reverence in African cultures, meditation in Eastern traditions, or psychotherapy in the West each provide pathways to wellness that are valid within their cultural contexts. If we ass counsellors impose our own cultural values without regard for these differences, we risk alienating clients and undermining the counselling relationship. Instead, by meeting clients within their cultural realities, we can offer support that feels respectful, relevant, and effective, helping clients to heal in ways that align with their identity, traditions, and lived experiences.

Cultural views of Mental Health

In Western psychology, mental health is often regarded in terms of disorders (for example, anxiety, depression, PTSD). In contrast, in South African and Chinese cultural contexts, mental health might be discussed in terms of *imbalance*, *disharmony*, or *communal healing*. For example:

In South Africa, especially among strong traditionalists, mental illness is often linked to spiritual imbalances or misalignments with ancestral traditions. I know this because I am South African. In China, based on my limited understanding, emotional and physical health is connected through the lens of *Qi* (vital life force) and *Yin-Yang* balance, which directly influences how mental health issues are perceived and addressed.

Practical Exercise: Cultural Mapping

I invite you to map your own cultural background and identify how it shapes your view of mental health. What are the common mental health terms in your culture? What models of healing are seen as "valid" or "effective"?

1.2 Cultural Perceptions of Mental Illness: Diverging Views Across Cultures

Effective counselling requires an understanding of cultural perspectives on mental health. In this section I will examine the conceptualization of mental disease in South African, Western, and Chinese contexts. In doing so, I believe it's critical to acknowledge that cultural beliefs influence how people perceive mental health issues, how they seek assistance, manage their discomfort, and react to solutions. By investigating these viewpoints, we can create culturally aware methods that honour customs and incorporate evidence-based procedures for comprehensive treatment.

South African Perspective:

Spiritual and Community Models: In many South African communities, mental illness is often viewed through a spiritual or communal lens. Issues such as depression, anxiety, or trauma are sometimes attributed to spiritual imbalances or disruptions in familial relationships.

Ubuntu (humanity/Interconnectedness): Our South African worldview emphasizes interconnectedness. *Ubuntu* means "I am because we are," which suggests that the well-being of the individual is inseparable from the community. Therefore, healing often involves group dynamics, collective rituals, and restoring harmonious relationships.

Traditional Healing: South Africa has a rich tradition of using ancestral knowledge and the guidance of *Sangomas* (traditional healers) to address mental health issues. In rural and urban contexts, some clients may seek counselling or guidance from these healers alongside or instead of Western-trained professionals.

Western perspective:

Biomedical and Psychological Models: These frameworks, which place an emphasis on diagnosis, pathology, and treatment with psychotherapy and/or medicine, are normally used to understand mental illness.

Autonomy and Individualism: Western cultures are more likely to place a strong emphasis on self-reliance and autonomy. Healing is frequently presented as an individual path emphasizing resilience, coping mechanisms, and self-awareness.

Evidence-Based Practice: With less emphasis on communal or spiritual aspects, counselling and therapy usually give priority to evidence-based interventions such cognitive behavioural therapy (CBT), trauma-informed approaches, and psychopharmacology.

Chinese perspective

Holistic and Balance Models: I tried to read a little bit on Chinese models and learned that with roots in theories like Taoism, Confucianism, and Traditional Chinese Medicine, mental health is frequently seen as an area of harmony and balance in the family, community, and body. Disturbances in family harmony or qi (vital energy) imbalances may be connected to emotional suffering. Which I found to be similar to South African perspectives in terms of being spiritually aware.

Collectivism and Social Harmony: Chinese culture places a strong emphasis on upholding social harmony, honouring elders, and fulfilling household responsibilities. Relationships and mental illness are frequently seen to be related, and family engagement is essential to comprehending and resolving issues.

Patterns of Stigma and Help-Seeking: Although there are psychiatric services available, people may be discouraged from getting professional assistance due to the stigma associated with mental illness. Instead, some people may use herbal medicine, spiritual activities, or traditional cures, either by themselves or in combination. Being based in China myself, I had to learn about the culture of 'face' and how it affects the Chinese people's worldview.

1.Case Study

Lindiwe, a 32-year-old South African woman, needs counselling after experiencing ongoing feelings of sadness and anxiety after the death of her father. She is certain her anxiety is linked to her *ancestral* spirits and their unresolved connection with her. The counsellor blends Western cognitive-behavioural techniques with elements of Ubuntu and spiritual healing, recommending community-based rituals for healing.

Reflection Prompt: How can a counsellor respect and integrate Lindiwe's belief in ancestral spirits while providing evidence-based practices such as CBT?

Case Overview

Client: Lindiwe, 32, South African woman

Presenting Issues: Persistent sadness and anxiety after father's death

Belief System: Links anxiety to ancestral spirits and unresolved spiritual connection

Counselor's Approach: Combines Western CBT, Ubuntu philosophy, and spiritual/community rituals.

Western Psychological Approach

Primary Focus:

The approach here would be one of evidence-based practice with a foundation on empirical research and psychological theories. This would help in terms of gaining insight into grief by using models like Worden's tasks of mourning or Kubler-Ross's phases of grief. The use of Cognitive Behavioral Therapy (CBT) would address anxiety in order to establish coping mechanisms and confront harmful thoughts.

Likely Interventions:

In my opinion, the following interventions might help: 1) psychoeducation about grief, trauma, and anxiety 2) Identifying and restructuring maladaptive thoughts (e.g., catastrophic thinking) 3) Relaxation and grounding techniques to manage anxiety symptoms and 4) Encouraging gradual re-engagement with daily life and support networks

View on Spiritual Beliefs:

A Western-trained psychologist may see belief in ancestral spirits as a cultural framework rather than an empirical truth. However, it is crucial to respectfully acknowledge the belief as meaningful to the client without necessarily validating it as a literal cause of symptoms.

African Healing Approach (Ubuntu & Indigenous Practices)

Primary Focus:

I believe the focus would include holistic healing rooted in the interconnectedness of self, family, ancestors, and community. In addition to this, South Africans believe that illness or distress is often understood as imbalance in spiritual, social, and physical realms. They also rely on the Ubuntu philosophy: "I am because we are" – personal well-being is tied to collective well-being.

Likely Interventions:

Most likely, I would assume that the interventions would be 1) ancestral rituals such as *ukuphahla* (communicating with ancestors through prayer and offerings) 2) Cleansing ceremonies to release emotional and spiritual burdens 3) Community-based support gatherings to reinforce belonging and shared grief processing 4) Guidance from a traditional healer (*sangoma*) to address the perceived ancestral disconnection.

View on Spiritual Beliefs:

This may not be true for all South Africans, but generally the belief in ancestral spirits is central and treated as real and impactful. In an ideal situation, the healer would work to directly restore harmony between the client and the ancestral realm.

Reflection Prompt Response

How to respect and integrate Lindiwe's belief in ancestral spirits while using CBT:

Cultural Validation: *Begin by affirming the importance of her belief system without dismissing it as superstition. This builds trust.*

Metaphor Integration: *Use CBT concepts in a way that aligns with her worldview—e.g., reframing intrusive anxious thoughts as "signals" from her inner self that need spiritual and emotional tending.*

Collaborative Healing Plan: *Encourage participation in ancestral rituals alongside CBT homework assignments (thought records, behavioral activation).*

Community Engagement: *Support her in accessing Ubuntu-based support structures such as family circles, community grief rituals, or traditional healers.*

Holistic Goal: *Make the therapy space one where evidence-based tools and cultural/spiritual healing reinforce each other rather than compete.*

2.Case Study:

John, a 28-year-old Western client, seeks counselling for panic attacks and chronic worry. The counsellor uses cognitive-behavioural therapy to help John recognize and challenge the irrational thoughts contributing to his anxiety. The therapist also teaches John relaxation techniques to regulate his emotional responses.

Reflection Prompt: How might John's focus on individual mental health, outside of family or community involvement, differ from a more communal approach like Ubuntu?

Case Overview

Client: John, 28, Western
Presenting Issues: Panic attacks and chronic worry
Therapist's Current Approach: CBT to challenge irrational thoughts + relaxation techniques for emotional regulation

Western Psychological Approach

Primary Focus:

The primary focus here is understanding anxiety as a result of maladaptive thought patterns and physiological responses. The emphasis would be on individual agency and self-management skills.

Likely Interventions:

The likely interventions would include: 1) Cognitive Restructuring: Identifying, challenging, and replacing irrational thoughts 2) Relaxation Techniques: Progressive muscle relaxation, deep breathing, guided imagery 3) Psychoeducation: Teaching about the fight-or-flight response and anxiety cycles and 4) Self-Monitoring: Thought logs, anxiety diaries.

View on Context:

The problem is primarily within John's cognition and behavior. For John, family or community involvement is optional and not essential, unless relevant to his preference.

African Healing Approach (Ubuntu Philosophy)

Primary Focus:

For South Africans, well-being is rooted in harmony between the individual, their community, and their ancestors. As a result, anxiety may be understood as a sign of disconnection from community, cultural values, or spiritual grounding.

Likely Interventions:

The likely interventions would include: 1) Communal Support: Group gatherings or talking circles to share experiences 2) Rituals: Ceremonies to restore balance and a sense of belonging 3) Mentorship: Guidance from elders or community leaders 4) Holistic Healing: Addressing social, emotional, and spiritual aspects together.

View on Context:

South Africans view healing as not just a personal journey; it involves restoring one's place in the collective fabric of life. In addition to this, mental health is a shared responsibility between the person and their community.

Reflection Prompt Response

How might John's individual focus differ from a communal Ubuntu approach?

Individualistic Focus (John's Western context):

Emphasis is on self-reliance, personal coping strategies, and internal cognitive change. Family or community may play a minimal role unless the client invites them in. The goal is personal symptom reduction and improved individual functioning.

Communal Focus (Ubuntu):

Emphasizes interconnectedness — mental health is tied to one's role and relationships within the community. Healing might include participation in communal activities, seeking guidance from elders, and engaging in rituals that reinforce belonging. Success is measured not only by personal symptom relief but by restoring harmony between self and community.

3.Case Study:

Wei, a 40-year-old Chinese client, seeks counselling for depression and fatigue. She has difficulty concentrating and sometimes feels disconnected from her family. Her counsellor integrates principles from both Western psychotherapy and Chinese traditional healing practices, introducing mindfulness meditation alongside suggestions for Tai Chi to restore her body's energy flow.

Reflection Prompt: How might Wei's cultural belief in the balance of *Qi* change the counsellor's counselling focus from simply addressing her emotions to exploring her body's energy and harmony?

Case Overview

Client: Wei, 40, Chinese
Presenting Issues: Depression, fatigue, concentration difficulties, feeling disconnected from family
Therapist's Current Approach: Combines Western psychotherapy with Chinese traditional healing — mindfulness meditation + Tai Chi to restore energy flow

Western Psychological Approach

Primary Focus:

For the West, depression is understood through cognitive, behavioral, and biological models — possibly linked to negative thought patterns, low motivation, and neurochemical imbalance. Fatigue and concentration issues are seen as symptoms of depressive disorder.

Likely Interventions:

The likely interventions here would include: 1) Cognitive-Behavioral Therapy (CBT): Challenging negative beliefs and promoting behavioral activation 2) Mindfulness-Based Cognitive Therapy (MBCT): Increasing present-moment awareness to reduce rumination 3) Lifestyle Adjustments: Sleep hygiene, exercise, balanced nutrition and 4) Psychoeducation: Understanding depression's physical and emotional components.

View on Context:

A western approach would suggest that emphasis is on individual coping skills and personal responsibility for recovery. Family relationships may be addressed, but the main focus is on the individual's inner experiences and behaviors.

Chinese Healing Approach

Primary Focus:

For Wei, depression and fatigue are viewed as signs of disrupted *Qi* flow and an imbalance between *yin* and *yang (darkness and light)*. Emotional distress is connected to organ systems (e.g., sadness linked to the Lungs, worry to the Spleen, fear to the Kidneys).

Likely Interventions:

The likely interventions would include: 1) Tai Chi (balance) & Qi Gong (energy): To improve energy circulation and restore harmony 2) Acupuncture & Herbal Medicine: To rebalance organ systems and replenish deficient Qi 3) Mindfulness & Breathwork: Enhancing awareness while regulating energy and calming the mind and 4) Family & Social Harmony: Encouraging family connection as a vital part of health.

View on Context:

In Wei's case, healing is a mind-body-spirit process, with physical energy balance being as important as emotional well-being. Her relationships and environment are key in sustaining Qi balance.

Reflection Prompt Response

How might Wei's cultural belief in Qi change the counselor's therapeutic focus?

Western Focus Alone: *Would likely center on mood, thought patterns, and behaviors affecting depression.*

Qi-Informed Focus: *Expands beyond emotions to consider how Wei's mental health is tied to physical energy, bodily harmony, and environment.*

Practical Shift:

-Therapy might include more body-based practices (Tai Chi, breathwork) alongside talk therapy.

-Assessment would involve exploring diet, sleep, physical movement, and environmental stressors as part of energy balance.

-Family connection would be encouraged as part of restoring Qi harmony, not just as emotional support.

1.3 The Intersection of counselling and Cultural Models: Possibilities and Difficulties

I will examine the difficulty of integrating different cultural frameworks into treatment in this section. It can be challenging to strike a balance between upholding cultural customs and using evidence-based psychological approaches. Counselors must cultivate cultural humility as a result of this integration, acknowledging the importance of indigenous knowledge systems while simultaneously utilizing contemporary counselling approaches. Ignoring clinical best practices may reduce the effectiveness of treatment, while disregarding cultural viewpoints may cause clients to become distrustful or disengaged. In order to foster acceptance and favorable mental health outcomes, practitioners must embrace a flexible, client-centered approach that honors cultural identity, integrates traditional methods when appropriate, and harmonizes them with evidence-based care.

Challenges in Integrating Models:

Cultural Conflict: Traditional African or Chinese ideas may occasionally conflict with Western psychological paradigms. For instance, a Western counselor may identify a client's symptoms of melancholy and exhaustion as major depressive illness, but the client's culture may interpret these symptoms as a transient spiritual or familial crisis.

Trust and Authenticity: People in some cultures may be hesitant to embrace Western counseling methods because they believe they are impersonal or at odds with their religious convictions. It takes cultural awareness, attentive listening, and a willingness to include alternative healing techniques to establish trust.

Practical Exercise:

I invite you to think about potential conflicts you've faced in integrating culturally diverse counselling methods. What cultural factors may have influenced the way you interacted with clients from different backgrounds?

Opportunities in Integration:

Holistic Healing: As counsellors we can provide a more comprehensive approach that takes into account the client's mental, emotional, physical, and spiritual well-being by combining South African, Western, and Chinese models. For instance, integrating Western counselling methods with the Chinese idea of Qi can offer a client who is struggling with chronic stress a whole healing experience.

Cultural Empowerment: Giving clients the chance to investigate their cultural identity and partake in healing techniques that are appropriate for their culture might enable them to take charge of their own recovery. This method promotes self-awareness and personal development in addition to validating the client's viewpoint.

African Case Study:

Mpho, a South African student in London, seeks counselling for stress and homesickness. The counsellor integrates CBT with storytelling, asking Mpho to share stories from her community that helped her feel connected to her roots. Mpho's healing involves reclaiming the communal practices of her home while learning coping mechanisms from Western counselling.

Reflection Prompt: How can integrating cultural practices in counselling help the client reconnect with their identity and heritage?

Western Case Study

Emma, a 25-year-old American graphic designer living in Cape Town, seeks counselling for anxiety related to her career and adapting to a new cultural environment. The counsellor uses CBT to help Emma identify her perfectionist thinking patterns and teaches her progressive muscle relaxation to manage anxiety symptoms. Recognizing Emma's cultural background, the counsellor also incorporates reflective journaling — a practice Emma grew up with through her family's tradition of keeping gratitude diaries. Emma's healing involves blending these personal rituals with structured CBT techniques, allowing her to ground herself in familiar values of self-reflection and goal setting while adapting to her new environment.

Reflection Prompt: How can therapists use familiar, culturally rooted personal practices to help expatriate clients adapt to new environments while managing mental health challenges?

Chinese Case Study

Li Mei, a 33-year-old teacher from Beijing living in Vancouver, seeks counseling for chronic fatigue and feelings of isolation. The counselor combines mindfulness-based stress reduction (MBSR) with traditional Chinese wellness practices. Li Mei is encouraged to practice daily mindfulness meditation while also integrating *Ba Duan Jin* (Eight Pieces of Brocade) Qigong exercises to restore her body's energy flow. In sessions, the counselor explores how Li Mei's sense of balance (*yin-yang*) has been disrupted by her fast-paced lifestyle and separation from her extended family. Her healing process involves reestablishing harmony in her daily routine through mindful movement, reconnecting with Chinese community groups in Vancouver, and applying Western therapeutic tools for emotional regulation.

Reflection Prompt: *How can blending evidence-based interventions with traditional practices rooted in Qi and balance enhance the cultural relevance and effectiveness of counselling?*

1.4 The Cultural Framework of the Counsellor

In my personal experience, the counsellor's cultural background has a significant impact on how treatment is delivered in counseling. The counsellors need to examine their own cultural prejudices and how they affect their therapeutic approach, which will be the main topic of this section. This is why I suggest that it is crucial to work on self-awareness since unconscious biases can influence a counselor's interpretation of symptoms, interactions with clients, and solution selection. Continuing cultural competency training, supervision, and reflective practice can all assist counsellors in recognizing and questioning their presumptions. By fostering cultural humility, counsellors provide room for clients' perspectives to be acknowledged, guaranteeing that the counselling alliance is based on mutual respect, understanding, and openness.

Self-Awareness and Cultural Humility:

Understanding the limitations of one's own cultural perspective and the value of learning from the client are two aspects of cultural humility. When combining models from other cultures, this humility is especially important. Cultural humility stresses a continuous process of self-reflection, openness, and willingness to adapt, in contrast to cultural competence, which can imply that one can totally "master" knowledge of another culture. Counselors must actively listen to their clients, affirm their lived experiences, and recognize any power dynamics that might be present in the therapeutic setting. The counsellor promotes cooperation and guarantees that treatment methods are not forced but rather co-created in ways that honor both cultural customs and psychological best practices by establishing the client as the authority on their own cultural identity.

Practical Exercise:

I invite you to complete a self-assessment of your own cultural identity and biases based on the following questions:

-"What cultural beliefs or practices do you hold strongly?"

-"How do you think these beliefs may influence your counselling style?"

-"How can you ensure you remain open to cultural diversity in your practice?"

Building Cultural Competence:

Counselors need to continuously improve their cultural competency, which entails studying various cultures and their distinct perspectives on mental health. Gaining expertise in ethnic counseling requires training, experience, and client feedback. Being culturally competent is a continuous process of development and adaptation rather than a one-time accomplishment. It necessitates being prepared to confront stereotypes, interact with people from other backgrounds, and keep up with the latest developments in cultural customs, values, and worldviews. Formal education, workshops, working with colleagues from many cultural backgrounds, and immersing oneself in various places to obtain personal knowledge are all ways to accomplish this. Making room for client feedback is equally crucial since it allows counselors to improve their methods and make sure that interventions are still appropriate, successful, and relevant in cross-cultural settings.

Reflection and Interactive Section

Lastly, I need you to complete the following reflection activities to deepen your understanding of how culture impacts psychological counselling:

Personal Reflection: How do you view mental health in your own culture? Are there aspects of your cultural view that may influence the way you approach counselling clients from different backgrounds?

Case Study Discussion: How would you approach a client who presents with a mental health issue that conflicts with your own cultural perspective? What approaches can you use to respect their cultural beliefs while providing effective treatment?

Chapter 2

Philosophical Foundations and Core Principles

2.1 The Role of Philosophy in Counselling

I'd like to believe that we can agree that a culture's perspective on the world is shaped by its philosophy. In addition to this we can further agree that philosophy affects our understanding of the self, the causes of pain, and the way to recovery in psychological counselling. The philosophical foundations of Chinese, Western, and South African psychological models will be examined in this chapter, along with how they affect therapeutic practice. These worldviews influence not only the definition of mental health but also what constitutes a successful or meaningful counselling outcome. For instance, Chinese philosophy places a strong emphasis on harmony, balance, and group responsibility, while South African traditions emphasize communal identity and spiritual connectedness.

Western philosophy, on the other hand, frequently emphasizes individual autonomy and rationality. Counselors can better understand why clients may have specific ideas about sickness, resilience, and recovery by looking at these philosophical underpinnings. This knowledge makes counselling more genuine and successful by enabling practitioners to modify sessions in ways that speak to clients' cultural values and life experiences.

Philosophy and Healing

In counselling, philosophy aids in defining what constitutes a "problem" and the means of achieving healing. Every cultural viewpoint offers a distinct perspective on human suffering and its solutions, whether the focus is on finding balance, achieving personal fulfillment, or re-establishing a connection with the community.

2.2 Ubuntu: Interconnectedness and Healing through Community

One of the most potent and applicable frameworks for psychological rehabilitation in South Africa, where I come from, is ubuntu, a concept that stresses communal connectivity. It centers on the notion that humans are essentially interconnected and that one's wellbeing is correlated with that of others. This perspective serves as a reminder to counsellors that relationships, family ties, and the larger community are all vital to healing. It is common to think of psychological anguish as both an individual experience and a disturbance of social peace. As a result, Ubuntu-inspired therapeutic approaches could involve family-based therapies, communal support groups, rituals of reconciliation, or collective practices. By incorporating Ubuntu into counseling, we as counsellors acknowledge the importance of empathy, solidarity, and shared responsibility while providing clients with a feeling of community that fosters holistic healing and resilience.

Ubuntu and the Self:

The fundamental assumption of Ubuntu is "I am, because we are." This demonstrates the idea that the community and the individual self are one and the same. Through the encouragement, participation, and support of others, healing and mental wellbeing are attained with an emphasis on the welfare of the group as a whole. This means that, in reality, personal issues are frequently discussed in the context of ancestry, family, and community rather than in isolation. A person's relationships with other people are fundamental to their identity, fortitude, and sense of purpose; it is frequently necessary to restore harmony and balance within these networks in order to heal. Adopting Ubuntu as a counselor means acknowledging the client's integration into their community, promoting ties of support, and assisting in the healing of broken bonds. Additionally, it emphasizes how crucial empathy, compassion, and a sense of shared humanity are as therapeutic tools.

In counselling, **Ubuntu** encourages: **Community Involvement:** Healing is often communal. A counsellor working from an Ubuntu perspective might encourage clients to seek support from their families, communities, or even engage in group counselling to restore balance. It also encourages **Collective Identity:** Helping clients reconnect with their community and ancestral roots can provide a sense of belonging, purpose, and emotional support.

Case Study:

Thabo, a South African man struggling with grief after losing his father, feels isolated and disconnected. His counsellor, using an Ubuntu framework, guides him to engage with his extended family and community, where collective rituals are performed to honour his father's legacy. Thabo finds comfort in these rituals, as they allow him to reconnect with his community and his identity.

Reflection Prompt: How might the inclusion of community rituals in counselling alter the healing process for clients experiencing grief?

Ubuntu in Practice:

Ubuntu's application in counselling may look like: 1) group sessions that foster a sense of community and shared experiences 2) the use of narrative therapy to help clients recount their stories, emphasizing the importance of community, family, and tradition and 3) encouraging group or family therapy as a means to restore balance and harmony within relationships.

Practical Exercise:

I invite you to reflect on the role of community in your own life and how it influences your mental well-being. Design a counselling exercise where a client reflects on their relationship with their family and community as part of their healing journey.

2.3 Western Models: The Philosophy of the Individual

Western psychological models are often founded on the concept of individualism. The pursuit of personal fulfilment, autonomy, and self-actualization is at the core of many Western counselling approaches. Philosophically, Western counselling tends to focus on the self as an independent, autonomous being capable of overcoming obstacles through self-reflection and personal responsibility.

Key Concepts

Individualism: In the West, mental health is often viewed as a personal responsibility. Counselling emphasizes individual agency, self-improvement, and problem-solving.

Humanism: Developed by Carl Rogers and others, humanistic therapy emphasizes self-actualization, personal growth, and the inherent potential for individuals to create meaningful lives.

Cognitive Behavioural Therapy (CBT): CBT is a therapeutic approach that challenges negative thought patterns and encourages individuals to take responsibility for changing their behaviours.

Western Healing through the Self:

In Western models, healing typically involves:

Self-Reflection: Techniques like journaling, introspection, and mindfulness are used to promote self-awareness.

Empowerment: Clients are seen as capable of achieving positive change through their own efforts, often with the counsellor acting as a guide.

Cognitive Reframing: Helping clients shift negative thought patterns to foster healthier perspectives.

Case Study:

Emily, a client experiencing depression and low self-esteem, seeks counselling in a Western context. Through CBT, she works to identify and reframe her negative thought patterns that centre around her self-worth. She learns to take responsibility for her thoughts and behaviour and develops coping strategies that empower her to navigate her depression.

Reflection Prompt: How does the emphasis on self-sufficiency in Western approaches shape Emily's understanding of her own mental health?

Application in Practice:

A counsellor using a Western approach might focus on individual goals and the development of coping strategies for personal growth. They might also encourage Emily to take ownership of her healing process. Lastly the counsellor might utilize structured methods such as goal setting, behaviour tracking, and cognitive restructuring.

Practical Exercise:

I invite you to explore the balance between self-reliance and community support in your own practice. How can Western approaches that focus on individual responsibility incorporate communal aspects without losing their essence?

2.4 Chinese Models: Harmony, Balance, and Holistic Healing

The Chinese philosophical view on mental health is rooted in holistic concepts such as **Yin and Yang** (the balance of opposites) and the flow of **Qi** (vital life energy). Chinese medicine and psychological practices focus on the interconnectedness of the mind, body, and spirit. Mental health is seen as the result of the balance or imbalance of energies within the body, and the healing process is often about restoring harmony.

Key Concepts

Yin and Yang: The dualistic philosophy that everything in life consists of opposing forces that are complementary. For example, the balance of Yin (passive, cool, feminine energy) and Yang (active, warm, masculine energy) is essential for mental and physical well-being.

Qi (Chi): Qi refers to the vital life force that flows through the body. Mental disturbances are seen as manifestations of blockages or imbalances in the flow of Qi.

The Five Elements: Wood, Fire, Earth, Metal, and Water are used to describe the cycles of energy that govern the body and mind. Each element corresponds to different emotions, organs, and seasons.

Chinese Healing Philosophy in Practice:

Holistic Approach: Counsellors working within the Chinese model would integrate physical health, emotions, and mental processes. The treatment could involve both psychological counselling and physical therapies like acupuncture, herbal medicine, or Qi Gong.

Balance of Yin and Yang: Counselling sessions may aim to balance the client's Yin and Yang, restoring equilibrium between emotional states like sadness (Yin) and anger (Yang).

Qi Flow and Emotional Health: The counsellor might focus on identifying energy blockages and recommending practices to restore the flow of Qi. Techniques like breathing exercises, acupuncture, or Tai Chi could be used alongside talk therapy.

Case Study:

Li Wei, a 45-year-old client from China, seeks counselling for anxiety and insomnia. Her counsellor, incorporating Chinese principles, explores how her work-life imbalance may be disrupting her Qi. The counsellor suggests mindfulness exercises and Qi Gong practices, while also using CBT to address her anxious thought patterns.

Reflection Prompt: How do the ideas of Qi and energy flow change the way a counsellor approaches mental health issues like anxiety?

Application in Practice:

Counsellors working within the Chinese framework might use somatic practices (e.g., Tai Chi or Qi Gong) to help clients release stored emotional tension. They might also encourage practices that support the flow of Qi, such as acupuncture or herbal remedies. Additionally, they might help clients align their emotional states with the natural cycles of life, such as focusing on rest during the Yin phase (night) and activity during the Yang phase (day).

Practical Exercise:

I invite you to create a counselling plan for a client using Chinese principles. How might you incorporate physical practices like Tai Chi or acupuncture into your work? How can you discuss these practices with clients who may be unfamiliar with them?

2.5 Integration of Philosophies: A Holistic Healing Framework

In this section I will examine how counselors might combine the fundamental ideas of Chinese healing, Western psychology, and Ubuntu into a cohesive therapy method. I believe that every one of these customs has special advantages: Chinese healing has an emphasis on balance, harmony, and the integration of mind, body, and spirit; Western psychology offers evidence-based techniques and structured models of care; and Ubuntu promotes interconnection and communal support. A unified approach would be one that weaves various viewpoints together in a way that is adaptable, considerate, and sensitive to the demands of the client rather than combining them into a single, inflexible framework. For instance, a counselor might combine Chinese mindfulness and balance-promoting activities with Ubuntu-inspired group discussions and Western methods like Cognitive Behavioral Therapy. We can develop culturally sensitive approaches that respect clients' identities and provide efficient, comprehensive care by using elements from each tradition.

Interconnectedness of Mind, Body, and Spirit:

In a fully integrative approach, the individual's community, physical health, and spiritual health are all taken into account in addition to their psychological state. A person's relationships with others are essential to their mental health, according to Ubuntu. The treatment procedure is informed by the principles of holistic health and energy balance found in Chinese philosophy. The emphasis on self-awareness, cognitive change, and individual empowerment in Western models is a potent healing tool.

Case Study:

Samantha, a 30-year-old South African woman, seeks counselling for chronic stress and depression. Her counsellor blends techniques from CBT to address cognitive distortions, encourages her to reconnect with her roots and community using Ubuntu, and suggests mindfulness practices from Chinese medicine to restore emotional balance and Qi flow.

Reflection Prompt: How might blending all three cultural frameworks—Ubuntu, Western, and Chinese—create a more comprehensive treatment plan?

Reflection and Interactive Section

To close this chapter, I invite you to reflect on your understanding of the core philosophical differences between South African, Western, and Chinese models:

Personal Reflection: How do your cultural beliefs shape your understanding of mental health? How might they influence your approach to counselling?

Practical Exercise: After considering the three models, design an integrative therapy session plan that incorporates aspects from Ubuntu, Western psychology, and Chinese philosophy. How would you approach a client experiencing grief from each cultural perspective?

Chapter 3

Integrating South African, Western, and Chinese Counselling Models

3.1 The Integrative Counselling Approach: Bridging Cultural Gaps

Thus far I can say, techniques from many therapy approaches are combined in an integrated counseling approach to produce a thorough, culturally aware practice. In this section I will look at how counselors might combine Chinese, Western, and South African approaches in ways that are both useful and considerate of the client's cultural heritage. Integration calls for serious consideration of the underlying values, ideologies, and worldviews that influence each approach; it goes beyond merely combining different techniques. A counselor might, for example, use Western evidence-based techniques like cognitive behavioral therapy (CBT) or trauma-informed care to provide structure and quantifiable results, integrate Chinese practices that emphasize balance, mindfulness, and the connection between the mind and body, and use Ubuntu principles to promote community-based healing. Counsellors may promote cultural identity, meet clients where they are, and avoid imposing a one-size-fits-all model because of this blending. In the end, an integrated approach should produce a versatile framework in which contemporary psychology and conventional wisdom enhance each other, leading to more comprehensive and successful treatment results.

Eclectic and Integrative Models

The integrative method is eclectic, which means that depending on the client's needs, cultural background, and current problems, therapists employ methods from several therapeutic schools of thought. Counselors can develop a more adaptable and dynamic framework for recovery by combining different approaches.

The Goal of Integration:

Integration is more than just mixing techniques; it's about developing a therapeutic approach that fits the client's values, beliefs, and worldview. In order to promote healing and development, it entails choosing the appropriate tools from each model according to the client's particular needs and circumstances.

3.2 Practical Techniques from the South African Model

It is important to note that the value of community, spirituality, and group healing are frequently emphasized in South African healing approaches. I have not used African practices in counselling, but as an African I know about the power of community. The cultural emphasis on connection and the counselling potential of shared experiences is reflected in these methods. Many approaches incorporate family members, peer groups, or community events into the treatment process rather than concentrating only on the person. Creating meaning, building resilience, and reestablishing harmony are common uses of storytelling, rituals, and ancestral traditions. Spirituality is important, and many clients turn to traditional healers like Sangomas or religious leaders in addition to counselors for advice. Through the integration of these traditions, South African counseling acknowledges the profound connection between spiritual beliefs and social networks and well-being. In order to ensure that treatment is in line with clients' daily circumstances, we as counselors must embrace a holistic perspective that values both psychological strategies and culturally based approaches to group healing.

Ubuntu-Inspired Counselling:

The ubuntu approach to counselling emphasizes relational dynamics, community, and group activity to assist recovery. To address relationship problems and bring peace back, the counselor may lead family or group counseling.

Techniques:

Group Sharing Circles: In order to strengthen the idea that people are interconnected, clients participate in group sharing or storytelling. Both emotional release and validation can be obtained from these circles.

Family or Community Involvement: To promote the person's wellbeing, the counsellor could suggest including members of the community or extended family in the healing process.

Cultural Rituals and Ceremonies: To respect customs and promote group healing, therapists occasionally include cultural rituals (such as ancestral offerings and communal healing techniques)

Case Study:

Khanyi, a 25-year-old woman, seeks counselling for emotional distress after a breakup. She feels disconnected from her family and community. The counsellor suggests engaging with her extended family, where a communal meal and storytelling can take place. Khanyi's sense of belonging is renewed, and the group shares wisdom and emotional support to help her process the pain of her breakup.

Reflection Prompt: How does a communal approach to healing differ from the individualistic approaches often seen in Western counselling?

Practical Exercise:

I invite you to design a group counselling session based on Ubuntu principles. What role does collective healing play in the session? How can clients benefit from group sharing or family involvement?

3.3 Practical Techniques from the Western Model

Western psychological models emphasize self-awareness, personal accountability, and cognitive restructuring, especially those based on cognitive-behavioral therapy (CBT) and humanistic treatment. I would say that based on literature, these models place a high value on a person's ability to identify and alter their thought patterns in order to enhance their emotional health. In order to promote good change, cognitive behavioral therapy (CBT) frequently combines behavioral exercises with the identification of distorted or unhelpful thoughts and their replacement with more adaptive, balanced thinking. Humanistic methods, on the other hand, promote a sense of agency and autonomy by emphasizing self-discovery, personal development, and potential realization. Essentially, I highlight that when combined, these strategies highlight how crucial it is for the patient to take an active part in their own recovery by promoting introspection, goal-setting, and problem-solving. Despite being extremely structured and grounded in data, these models may be modified to take cultural context into account, guaranteeing that interventions stay pertinent and considerate of the client's perspective.

Cognitive-Behavioural Therapy (CBT):

The goal of cognitive behavioral therapy is to recognize harmful thought patterns and swap them out for more sensible, balanced ideas. For problems like anxiety, depression, and trauma, it works especially well because it enables clients to understand how faulty thinking fuels emotional suffering and unhelpful behavior. Clients are empowered to actively confront harmful ideas and create better coping mechanisms via the use of structured tools such thought journals, cognitive reframing, behavioral experiments, and skills training. CBT gives clients useful tools to control symptoms in day-to-day living by emphasizing goal-setting and quantifiable improvement. CBT is a versatile technique for a variety of groups, even though it was initially created in Western contexts. By incorporating clients' beliefs, social dynamics, and spiritual viewpoints into the cognitive and behavioral framework, it can be modified to respect cultural values.

Techniques:

Cognitive restructuring: helping clients recognize and confront illogical or pessimistic beliefs and swap them out for more sensible, constructive ones is known as cognitive restructuring.

Behavioural Activation: To interrupt the cycle of sadness, clients are encouraged to partake in enjoyable activities or activities that give them a sense of achievement.

Thought journals: to encourage introspection and transformation, clients keep thought journals in which they record negative ideas and evaluate the facts supporting and refuting them.

Case Study:

Tom, a 38-year-old man, is dealing with chronic anxiety and panic attacks. His counsellor uses CBT to help him identify the automatic negative thoughts that trigger his anxiety (e.g., "I'm going to fail at work"). The counsellor teaches Tom to reframe his thoughts (e.g., "I have the skills to manage challenges, and I can ask for support when needed"). Over time, Tom learns to manage his anxiety through this cognitive restructuring process.

Reflection Prompt: How can CBT be adapted to better suit a client who values communal support or spiritual healing, as seen in other cultural models?

Practical Exercise:

I invite you to create a sample thought record for a client struggling with negative thinking. How can the counsellor guide the client in identifying cognitive distortions and replacing them with healthier thoughts?

3.4 Practical Techniques from the Chinese Model

After some reading, I learned that the concepts of energy flow (Qi), balance, and the mind-body connection are all incorporated into the Chinese counselling model. This, I understand, is a holistic approach to mental health which places a strong emphasis on reestablishing equilibrium among the body, mind, and spirit. A disturbance in this balance is commonly seen as psychological discomfort, which can show itself as social, emotional, or physical symptoms. Furthermore, acupuncture, herbal medicine, Tai Chi, Qigong, and mindfulness are all part of traditional Chinese methods to balance energy flow and promote general health. Like South African models in terms of collectivism, a collectivist worldview for Chinese practices also views family, social peace, and conformity to cultural standards as essential components of mental health. In the context of counseling, these guidelines support interventions that foster balance, build resilience, and reinforce the connections between social, familial, and personal life. The Chinese model provides a thorough and culturally relevant framework for fostering mental wellness by addressing both psychological and physical aspects.

Mindfulness and Qi Practices:

Chinese counselling practices often incorporate mindfulness, Qi Gong, Tai Chi, acupuncture, and herbal remedies to restore emotional and physical balance. Let us get into more details about them:

Techniques:

Qi Gong: A method of breathing, meditation, and coordinated body movements intended to balance the body's Qi (energy flow). Counsellors can help clients who are experiencing stress, anxiety, or emotional blocks by introducing them to Qi Gong activities.

Mindfulness Meditation: This Buddhist-based technique assists clients in developing present-moment awareness and letting go of negative thought patterns.

Acupuncture and Acupressure: Although these treatments are frequently administered by qualified professionals, counsellors may suggest relaxation methods or acupressure to help Qi flow again.

Case Study:

Li Hua, a 50-year-old woman from China, struggles with insomnia and high stress due to work pressures. Her counsellor suggests a combination of mindfulness meditation and Tai Chi to help regulate her energy levels. The counsellor also incorporates cognitive strategies to manage her anxious thoughts about work. Over several sessions, Li Hua learns to calm her mind and restore balance through mindful movement and meditation.

Reflection Prompt: How might the integration of physical practices like Tai Chi and acupuncture enhance a client's emotional well-being?

Practical Exercise:

I invite you to design a mindfulness meditation practice that could be integrated into a session for a client dealing with stress or emotional imbalance. How does mindfulness help restore balance and reduce mental tension?

3.5 Integrating Techniques in a Single Therapeutic Framework

When we want to integrate techniques, the client's particular demands and worldview must be carefully considered when integrating tactics from all three cultural paradigms. In actuality, an integrative counsellor will choose techniques according to the client's cultural background, current problem, and treatment objectives. This entails knowing the underlying values and attitudes that guide each method in addition to selecting the right solutions. A counsellor might, for instance, use CBT techniques to address negative thought patterns, integrate Chinese mindfulness or balance practices to enhance overall well-being, and use Ubuntu-inspired family or community support to strengthen relational bonds. Since the counselor is always assessing what is respectful and effective, flexibility, cultural humility, and constant communication with the client are crucial. Practitioners can offer a person-centered, culturally sensitive treatment experience that can address the intricate interactions between psychological, social, and spiritual aspects of the client's life by carefully combining different approaches. I personally use a lot of mindfulness alongside western counselling.

Key Considerations for Integration:

Cultural Sensitivity: Make sure the client is at ease with the therapeutic approaches being used at all times. For example, whereas a Western client might Favor more structured, individual-focused approaches like cognitive behavioural therapy, a South African client might feel more comfortable with family engagement and communal rituals.

Flexibility: As the counselling process develops, the counsellor should continue to be adaptable and open to using various techniques. For instance, before switching to more individualized techniques like CBT, a client who first struggles with personal responsibility can find that the communal and spiritual elements of Ubuntu are beneficial.

Holistic View: Using a holistic approach entails striking a balance between spiritual, physical, emotional, and cognitive disciplines. Combining Chinese mindfulness techniques, South African communal healing, and Western cognitive restructuring may improve a client's mental health.

Case Study:

Amina, a 30-year-old woman from Johannesburg, seeks counselling for chronic stress and anxiety following a difficult breakup.

Her counsellor takes an integrative approach by using CBT to help Amina challenge her negative self-talk and regain emotional control. The counsellor also encourages Amina to reconnect with her roots and participate in a family healing ritual to restore her sense of community and support. Lastly, the counsellor Introduces mindfulness practices from the Chinese model, such as deep breathing and meditation, to help Amina manage anxiety in the present moment.

Through this integrative approach, Amina experiences relief from her stress, gains insight into her emotional patterns, and reestablishes her connection to both her and her community.

Reflection Prompt: How can integrating different models in counselling provide a more comprehensive solution to a client's complex, multi-dimensional needs?

Reflection and Interactive Section

At the end of this chapter, I encourage you to engage in the following reflective activities:

Personal Reflection: How do you see yourself as a counsellor in terms of integrating cultural models? What would an integrative approach look like in your practice? Consider a case where you might blend Western, South African, and Chinese models (or cultures you're exposed to).

Practical Exercise: Design a counselling plan for a client with a complex issue (e.g., grief, anxiety, or trauma) that integrates all three cultural approaches. What methods will you use from each model, and how will they complement each other in the healing process?

Chapter 4

Assessing and Adapting Counselling Models to Clients' Needs

4.1 The Importance of Culturally Informed Assessments

A fundamental first step in making sure your selected counselling style fits the client's requirements, values, and worldview is conducting an efficient assessment. I usually use a very thorough and holistic assessment just to make sure that I do indeed create a safe space for my clients. For the treatment to be successful, it is crucial to evaluate the client's cultural background, current problems, and level of preparedness for various counselling approaches. In addition to the usual intake paperwork and symptom checklists, this procedure involves discussions on values, spiritual beliefs, family dynamics, and prior experiences receiving mental health treatment. Being sensitive to cultural differences when examining the client's knowledge of mental health, coping mechanisms, and attitudes toward different therapy models—whether Western, South African, or Chinese—may be part of the diagnostic process. In order to provide a secure environment where the client feels heard and acknowledged, the therapist must also be conscious of their own prejudices. Counsellors can provide respectful and pertinent counselling sessions that boost participation, trust, and the possibility of significant counselling success by customizing assessments to each client's cultural and psychological background.

Culturally Responsive Assessment

Understanding and honoring the client's cultural identity, values, and worldview while determining the best counselling strategy is known as culturally responsive evaluation. It includes: 1) being aware of the cultural background and experiences of the client 2) investigating how the client's understanding of their problems is influenced by cultural elements like community, family dynamics, spirituality, and societal expectations and 3) determining the client's counselling preferences and goals.

Why This Matters in Integrative Therapy:

I personally believe that an integrative model necessitates adaptability. The counsellor can determine which therapy techniques will be most effective for a client and which may be unfamiliar or unsettling by evaluating the client's cultural background. Actively listening to the client's experiences, convictions, and preferences is a necessary part of this process, as is being prepared to modify conventional methods to fit their perspective. For instance, in accordance with Ubuntu ideals, a counsellor can adapt cognitive-behavioral exercises to include input from family or the community, or they might use mindfulness and balance techniques influenced by Chinese philosophy in addition to Western approaches. Being flexible also entails asking for feedback, keeping an eye on how the client reacts to various approaches, and modifying the treatment plan iteratively. Counsellors who maintain their flexibility and openness foster a collaborative environment that develops therapeutic rapport, supports the client's cultural identity, and increases the intervention's overall efficacy and relevance.

4.2 Conducting a Culturally Sensitive Assessment

Before starting counselling, as I discussed earlier, a comprehensive evaluation that considers the client's cultural background and psychological needs must be carried out. This is more culture specific as compared to the earlier discussion in 4.1, its more thorough and has steps that guide the assessment. Let us examine the procedure more carefully. Finding out about the client's cultural background, family relationships, spiritual beliefs, and social surroundings is just as important as learning about their symptoms, mental health history, and current problems. Knowing these elements enables the counselor to predict which therapy modalities are likely to work and which would require modification. Culturally sensitive surveys, structured interviews, and open-ended discussions that let clients express their counselling preferences and worldview are all possible components of the assessment process. Counsellors can create a treatment plan that is individualized, respectful, and in line with the client's values by incorporating psychological and cultural factors early on. This will set the stage for a more successful and engaging counselling experience.

Step 1: Building Cultural Awareness

As counsellors we should begin by developing cultural awareness through: 1) Inquiring open-endedly about the client's values, beliefs, and cultural background 2) being aware of how cultural elements like gender, ethnicity, class, and religion affect the client's experiences and 3) Understanding that clients may view issues differently and that there are several approaches to counselling.

Step 2: Understanding the Client's Worldview

It's important for us to understand how the client views their problems. This can involve: 1) understanding whether the client believes the problem is individual, relational, or spiritual 2) exploring how the client views mental health and healing within the context of their cultural traditions and lastly, using culturally appropriate language and metaphors to ensure effective communication.

Step 3: Identifying the Client's Readiness for Change

Understanding the client's readiness to engage with different counselling methods is crucial. For example: 1) some clients may be more open to Western models like CBT because of their structured, goal-oriented nature 2) others may prefer South African communal healing practices or Chinese mindfulness approaches or 3) some clients may resist unfamiliar practices, especially if they do not align with their cultural or personal beliefs.

African Case Study:

Lindiwe, a 40-year-old South African woman, seeks counselling after a difficult divorce. Her cultural background emphasizes communal values and spirituality. When assessing her, the counsellor asks questions about her relationship with her extended family and her spiritual beliefs. Lindiwe reveals that her community and ancestral rituals play a central role in her understanding of healing. The counsellor recognizes that incorporating these aspects into counselling will be essential to her emotional recovery.

Reflection Prompt: How can the counsellor's awareness of Lindiwe's community and spiritual practices influence the counselling process?

Western Case Study

Michael, a 42-year-old Canadian man, seeks counselling after a difficult divorce. Raised in a culture that emphasizes individual autonomy and self-reliance, Michael initially approaches therapy with a focus on personal coping strategies rather than community or family involvement. When assessing him, the counselor asks about his support system, personal values, and past strategies for managing stress. Michael explains that he finds meaning in self-reflection, journaling, and pursuing personal hobbies like hiking and photography. The counselor recognizes that incorporating these personal, individual-focused coping methods alongside structured CBT techniques will be key to helping Michael regain emotional stability and independence.

Reflection Prompt: How can the counselor's awareness of Michael's value of self-reliance and individual coping strategies shape the choice of therapeutic techniques?

Chinese Case Study

Zhang Wei, a 40-year-old woman from Shanghai, seeks counselling after a difficult divorce. Her cultural background emphasizes family harmony, balance, and respect for tradition. During the assessment, the counsellor explores her relationship with her family, her beliefs about yin-yang balance, and her views on life transitions. Zhang Wei shares that she has been feeling emotionally drained and believes her qi (energy) has been disrupted. She mentions that practicing Tai Chi and visiting temples to burn incense are part of her personal healing rituals. The counselor recognizes that blending evidence-based approaches such as mindfulness-based cognitive therapy with traditional practices aimed at restoring qi will be essential for her emotional recovery.

Reflection Prompt: How can the counselor's awareness of Zhang Wei's belief in energy balance and her traditional healing rituals guide the integration of therapeutic methods?

Practical Exercise:

I invite you to create a list of open-ended questions that you might ask clients to assess their readiness for change, particularly in terms of integrating different cultural models.

4.3 Adapting the Counselling Models Based on the Assessment

Once you as the counsellor would have conducted a culturally sensitive assessment, you can adapt your counselling approach based on the client's specific needs. Let's look at how different counselling models can be adapted based on the assessment.

Adapting the South African Model: Ubuntu and Community Healing

South African clients who value communal relationships and collective healing can benefit from approaches that focus on group dynamics, social support, and spiritual practices.

Adaptation Tips:

Involve Family or Community: If the client has strong family or community ties, therapy might include sessions with family members or group counselling. This could help restore the sense of connection that is vital to their well-being.

Emphasize Spirituality and Rituals: For clients who draw strength from spiritual or ancestral practices, the therapist could include rituals (e.g., ancestor veneration, communal prayers) as part of the healing process.

Healing through Storytelling: Encourage clients to share their stories, as storytelling is often an important aspect of cultural healing. This allows the client to express their pain and process emotions in a way that resonates with their cultural traditions.

Case Study:

Mbali, a young woman from a rural South African village, experiences depression following the loss of her mother. She struggles to cope with the loss on her own but feels supported when her therapist suggests involving her extended family in the healing process. They engage in traditional healing practices, and Mbali begins to find solace in community support and ritual.

Reflection Prompt: How might Mbali's cultural context influence her experience of grief? How can you support her through a process that respects her cultural norms?

Adapting the Western Model: Cognitive Behavioural Therapy (CBT)

Generally, I believe many clients may benefit from Western therapeutic approaches that emphasize personal development, introspection, and self-determination, particularly those from more individualistic countries. These methods prioritize the autonomy of the client, motivating them to actively participate in recognizing obstacles, establishing objectives, and putting change-related strategies into action. Methods like humanistic therapy, cognitive behavioral therapy (CBT), and solution-focused approaches enable clients to analyze their thoughts, feelings, and behaviors in a methodical manner, fostering self-awareness and skill improvement. Clients with individualistic tendencies frequently cherish the chance to develop their sense of self, make choices on their own, and make quantifiable clinical improvement. Counsellors can facilitate significant personal transformation, increase motivation, and improve participation by integrating counselling approaches with these cultural values.

On the other hand, while seeking counselling, clients from collectivist cultures—like many Chinese or South African communities—may place more value on societal harmony, family, and connections. For these clients, mental health is frequently seen as a family or community issue rather than a personal one. It may be more effective to use therapeutic approaches that include family involvement, group support, or culturally grounded practices, such Chinese balance and mindfulness techniques or Ubuntu-based counselling. As stressed in Western models, concentrating only on self-reflection or individual empowerment may feel strange or even alienating. Counselors who are aware of these cultural variations can modify their interventions to respect the client's values, incorporate pertinent cultural customs, and establish a therapy setting that is both productive and courteous.

Adaptation Tips:

Focus on Self-Empowerment: Here clients can be encouraged to set clear, achievable goals and provide them with the tools to address their own issues.

Introduce Mindfulness Practices: Even in Western CBT, mindfulness techniques can be integrated to help clients stay present and avoid reflecting on negative thoughts. Like I said earlier, I have tried this.

Incorporate Strengths-Based Approaches: In Western counselling, a strengths-based perspective focuses on the client's inherent abilities. Helping clients identify and leverage their strengths can foster resilience and empowerment.

Case Study:

John, an American client, seeks counselling to address his struggle with anxiety and job stress. His therapist uses CBT to help John identify his automatic negative thoughts and reframe them into more balanced, positive thoughts. John appreciates the goal-oriented nature of this approach, and his anxiety improves as he becomes more aware of his thinking patterns.

Reflection Prompt: How does the goal-oriented nature of CBT resonate with John's cultural background? How does his individualistic perspective influence the counselling process?

Adapting the Chinese Model: Mind-Body Connection and Qi

A common theme in Chinese therapeutic methods is the harmony of the mind, body, and spirit. Counsellors can use Qi Gong, mindfulness, and other energy-focused therapies with clients who appreciate holistic approaches to health and recovery.

Adaptation Tips:

Focus on Balance and Harmony: This can be done by working with clients to restore emotional and physical balance by teaching them about Qi, the flow of life energy, and how it impacts mental health.
Introduce Mindfulness and Meditation: Encourage practices like Tai Chi or mindfulness meditation to help clients centre themselves and become aware of the present moment.
Use Symbolism and Metaphors: In Chinese therapy, metaphors like the balance of Yin and Yang, the Five Elements, and Qi can be used to help clients understand their emotional states and mental health issues.

Case Study:

Wei, a 35-year-old client from China, seeks help for chronic fatigue and stress. His counsellor incorporates Qi Gong exercises to help Wei restore balance and flow in his body, while also addressing negative thought patterns through a combination of CBT and Chinese philosophy. Wei feels a sense of renewal and begins to understand his stress as a result of blocked energy in his body.

Reflection Prompt: How might the integration of Qi Gong and mindfulness practices be particularly beneficial for a client like Wei? How does his understanding of stress differ from more traditional Western approaches?

4.4 Strategies for Integrating Assessment into Ongoing Counselling

As most counsellors should already know, the intake session is only the beginning of an effective evaluation. As the counselling goes on, it ought to be a continuous process that changes. The counsellor can keep an eye on how the client's mental health changes, assess how well sessions work, and modify tactics to better suit the client's requirements by conducting ongoing assessments. Additionally, it offers chances to reevaluate cultural factors, guaranteeing that counselling techniques stay appropriate and pertinent as the client's knowledge and comfort level with various approaches increase. The following are methods for incorporating evaluation into the treatment process:

Regular Check-Ins: During each session, counsellors should revisit the client's cultural and personal goals for therapy to ensure that the approach remains aligned with the client's evolving needs.

Client Feedback: Counsellors should ask clients for feedback on how they feel the therapy is progressing. This allows the counsellor to adapt the treatment plan as necessary.

Adapting Based on Progress: As the client progresses, counselling sessions may reveal that certain methods from South African, Western, or Chinese models are more or less effective. Continuously assessing the client's responses and needs will guide the counsellor in making necessary adjustments.

Reflection and Interactive Section

At the end of this chapter, I encourage you engage in the following activities to deepen your understanding:

Personal Reflection: Reflect on a client you've worked with in the past. How did you assess their cultural background and needs? How did that influence your choice of counselling techniques? Would you have done anything differently with the knowledge gained in this chapter?

Practical Exercise:

I invite you to conduct a mock assessment. Select a hypothetical client, considering their cultural background, presenting issues, and readiness for change. Design a therapeutic approach that integrates elements from South African, Western, and Chinese models. How will you adapt each model to fit this client's unique needs?

Chapter 5

Practical Case Studies in Integrated Counselling

In this chapter I will focus on putting theory into practice. I will propose a broad and diverse toolkit by the combination of Western, South African, and Chinese therapeutic models. Nevertheless, the real test is how well these approaches are applied in practical settings. While keeping an adaptable, client-centered approach, counsellors must negotiate the interaction of cultural values, personal views, and individual psychological needs. I will provide case studies that show how counsellors might deal with these difficulties by choosing and modifying solutions that align with the client's goals, presenting concerns, and cultural background. Each case illustrates the theory's practical implementation by highlighting the intentional blending of concepts like Chinese practices that prioritize balance and mindfulness, Western evidence-based methods, and Ubuntu-inspired communal assistance.

These examples demonstrate the flexibility of an integrated approach as well as the value of continuous evaluation, cultural humility, and reflective practice in delivering comprehensive, successful, and culturally aware psychological care. We as counsellors can learn more about the complex choices and adjustments needed to convert integrative frameworks into significant treatment results by looking at these examples. In order to ensure that treatment is not only theoretically sensible but also applicable, courteous, and powerful in practice, they also emphasize the importance of customizing interventions to meet the particular requirements of each client.

Case Study 1: Integrating Western Cognitive Behavioural Therapy (CBT) with Ubuntu and Chinese Daoist Principles

Client profile

Sarah is a 28-year-old South African woman, living in Johannesburg, who struggles with anxiety and self-doubt. Raised in a predominantly Western-leaning educational environment, she feels disconnected from her cultural roots. She often experiences a constant sense of pressure, both professionally and socially, to "succeed" according to a Westernized definition of achievement. Despite this, Sarah frequently finds herself yearning for a deeper sense of purpose and connection to her heritage.

Therapeutic Approach:

Western Model: To treat Sarah's anxiety, we start with Cognitive Behavioural Therapy (CBT) techniques. We focus on her negative thought patterns, which can lead to tension and feelings of inadequacy.

South African Ubuntu Model: We provide Ubuntu values during sessions, stressing the importance of connections, community, and interconnectedness as key components of her recovery. This method encourages Sarah to consider her place in the community and how her support networks and relationships contribute to her sense of value.

Chinese Daoist Model: The principle of balance, or yin-yang, is fundamental to Daoism. We examine Sarah's internal struggle between achieving personal achievement and fostering harmony with others, helping her to find balance in her life by relating to both her own goals and the general welfare of her neighbourhood.

Outcomes:

When we combine these strategies, we can expect them to give Sarah the confidence to see the importance of her own achievements as well as her place in her larger social network. The incorporation of Ubuntu promotes a more comprehensive view of achievement by assisting her in rediscovering her identity and roots. She can control her worry by comprehending the flow of existence, which lowers stress and promotes a deeper sense of tranquility, according to the Daoist emphasis on balance.

Case Study 2: Working with a Chinese Immigrant Family Using South African and Western Family Counselling Approaches

Client Profile:

Li Mei and her husband, Chen, are recent immigrants to South Africa from China. They have two children, ages 6 and 9. Li Mei is experiencing difficulty adjusting to her new life in South Africa, particularly in balancing the expectations of her traditional Chinese upbringing with the Western ideals of independence and individualism that seem to be influencing her children's behaviour. Chen, on the other hand, feels that his wife is overreacting and prefers to maintain a more "hands-off" approach to parenting.

Counselling Approach:

Western Model: To highlight patterns of behaviour and communication within the family dynamic, we apply a Family Systems Therapy method. The objective is to assist each family member in understanding their functions within the system and how their actions affect the family as a whole.

South African Ubuntu Model: We include Ubuntu's communal ideals to highlight the significance of shared responsibility, respect, and interdependence within the family. This method aids Li Mei and Chen in realizing that the family is a community in which the welfare of every member is interrelated and that the interaction dynamics within the family should be taken into consideration when interpreting the behaviour of the children.

Chinese Model: We also include elements of Confucian family values, emphasizing the value of preserving family harmony, filial piety, and respect for elders. These principles are examined in light of Li Mei's cultural viewpoint and her wish to support her kids in acclimating to their new surroundings while upholding family customs.

Outcomes:

By using this integrated approach, Li Mei starts to see how her cultural heritage and her new surroundings affect her aspirations for her kids. The Chinese value of respecting elders and the Western impact of fostering children's independence can be balanced by the family. As a result, parenting becomes more adaptable and encouraging, honoring Li Mei's cultural background as well as her family's requirements in their new cultural setting.

Case Study 3: Using South African Traditional Healing, Western Trauma-Informed Counselling, and Chinese Qi Gong for a Refugee Client

Client Profile:

Abdi, a 34-year-old refugee from Somalia, has been living in South Africa for the past two years. He survived significant trauma, including witnessing violence and losing family members. Although he sought asylum, his trauma and sense of displacement continue to affect his mental health, manifesting in post-traumatic stress disorder (PTSD) symptoms such as nightmares, hypervigilance, and detachment.

Counselling Approach:

Western Model: To make Abdi feel comfortable and supported, we start by applying the concepts of trauma-informed therapy. His PTSD symptoms are treated with cognitive processing therapy (CPT), which aims to reframe the horrific memories and include the event into his story without overwhelming him.

South African Traditional Healing: We incorporate a spiritual component into the therapy in acknowledgment of Abdi's Somali heritage and the pervasive usage of traditional healers in his community. For spiritual support and rituals to help Abdi re-establish a link with his ancestors—which may be restorative for someone who has suffered such a great loss—we visit with a local healer, a revered elder in the community.

Chinese Model: Abdi is given Qi Gong as a way to help him balance and control the qi in his body. Abdi discovers how to focus on his breathing, lower stress levels, and encourage healing via movement and awareness by engaging in Qi Gong. His physical and mental healing is supported by the comprehensive approach created by this technique in conjunction with trauma-informed treatment.

Outcomes:

Abdi starts to report that his PTSD symptoms are lessening. He can process his pain in an organized way with trauma-informed treatment, and he feels closer to his culture and history thanks to the incorporation of traditional healing techniques. He can relax and control his body's physical reactions to stress thanks to Qi Gong. As time goes on, Abdi feels more empowered and hopeful because she realizes that recovery is achievable when ancient methods are combined with contemporary counselling techniques.

Reflections on the Case Studies

I hope that these case studies show how effective it is to combine Chinese, South African, and Western paradigms into a unified, flexible therapy approach. Ideally my goal here is that they emphasize that there is no one-size-fits-all approach to psychological healing and that effective therapy requires cultural sensitivity, adaptability, and a thorough comprehension of each client's particular requirements and experience. As practitioners we can recognize the benefits of integrating evidence-based methods, group and spiritual approaches, and holistic mind-body activities by looking at how these various frameworks can enhance one another. Providing a flexible toolkit that can be adjusted to the client's perspective in order to foster resilience, well-being, and meaningful participation is my main aim. It is important to note that this does not imply that these models are exclusive to clients from these three cultures. Rather, through this book I aim to push practitioners to consider their approach to clients from any cultural background more carefully and critically, promoting creativity and cultural humility in all therapeutic interactions.

My stance is that fact that each client is different means that the integration of these models needs to be handled with consideration, care, and constant introspection. Although the examples show how these frameworks can be used practically, counsellors should feel free to modify interventions according to the requirements, preferences, and circumstances of each client. I hope that this method guarantees that therapy stays effective, meaningful, and culturally appropriate by promoting ongoing learning and response. Practitioners can develop interventions that respect the client's identity, validate their experiences, and promote holistic healing across many cultural landscapes by carefully combining insights from several traditions.

Chapter 6

The Role of the Counsellor in an Integrated Counselling Approach

As I have discussed, a counsellor's capacity to address the various needs of their clients can be substantially improved by incorporating Western, South African, and Chinese therapeutic models into their counseling practices. South African viewpoints stress relational connection, spirituality, and community support; Chinese models promote balance, mindfulness, and holistic well-being; while Western models offer organized, evidence-based techniques. I believe that each framework has its own advantages. But how the counsellor integrates these approaches and tailors them to particular client situations while upholding a client-centered, ethical, and considerate approach is the true test. This calls for not only technical expertise in various approaches but also self-awareness, cultural humility, and the capacity to adapt to the changing requirements of the client.

We will explore the abilities, traits, and difficulties that counsellors may encounter while putting an integrated therapeutic model into practice in this chapter. Practical methods for combining various approaches, methods for evaluating and attending to culturally complex client demands, and tactics for upholding ethical standards when negotiating different worldviews will all be covered. We'll also look at typical issues including handling cultural misunderstandings, striking a balance between conventional and contemporary approaches, and resolving conflicting client and therapist expectations. By examining these topics, the chapter hopes to give professionals practical skills and insights to successfully implement integrative, culturally sensitive counseling while promoting cooperation, trust, and significant therapeutic results.

1. Cultural Competence: Going Beyond Knowledge to Application

In my little knowledge and experience, I believe that understanding cultural norms is only one aspect of cultural competency, which is crucial when using an integrated approach. Another is integrating this information to the counselling process in a way that respects and accepts the client's lived experience. This involves identifying how the client's cultural background influences their views on mental health, coping mechanisms, familial relationships, and the whole concept of healing. Throughout the counselling relationship, counsellors must be open to learning from their clients and actively reflect on their own prejudices, presumptions, and potential blind spots.

Additionally, we should know that adapting interventions to be meaningful and relevant also involves being culturally competent. This can include modifying communication approaches to respect cultural norms, integrating family or community support, or matching methods with philosophical or spiritual frameworks. Last but not least, counsellors can establish a secure, affirming, and productive environment for clients from a variety of backgrounds by combining their expertise, humility, and practical application.

The Depth of Cultural Competence:

Deep Cultural Knowledge: In addition to comprehending the general traits of various cultures (such as South African communal values, Chinese family roles, and Western individualistic emphasis), a culturally competent therapist must also be aware of how these cultural norms appear in the particular context of the client's life. This calls for ongoing education regarding the subtleties of various customs, methods of treatment, and worldviews.

Contextualizing Cultural Knowledge: A therapist should be able to evaluate the ways in which a client's culture influences their difficulties and experiences. For instance, even though they belong to the same ethnic group, a South African customer who was reared in an urban context can have a totally different cultural experience than one who was raised in a rural one. Similar distinctions may exist within Chinese culture between those who adhere to more traditional Confucian ideas and those who identify with a more modernized perspective of the family and the self, or between urban and rural values.

Practical Application of Cultural Competence:

Personalizing Techniques: When working with a Chinese client, for instance, a therapist can discover that methods that respect hierarchy and family relations are more meaningful than Western approaches that place an emphasis on individuality. A counselling intervention that emphasizes community and collective healing, on the other hand, can seem more pertinent to a South African client who is influenced by the Ubuntu ideology than purely individualistic models.

Cultural Adaptability: The counselling relationship may be weakened by cultural presumptions, so counsellors should refrain from "cultural stereotyping." Rather, we must openly discuss cultural identity with our clients and adjust our approaches accordingly. Open-ended questions like "How does your cultural background influence how you cope with stress?" can be used to encourage clients to reveal their cultural norms, beliefs, and values.

2. Flexibility and Adaptability: Crafting the Counselling to Fit the Client

I would like to suggest that when employing an integrated approach, flexibility is fundamental. Instead of imposing a strict counselling approach, we must customize interventions to the particular circumstances of each client. The cultural, societal, and personal elements that each client brings to the table impact how they feel distress and view recovery. Allowing your approach to remain adaptable allows you as the counsellor to modify the application of Chinese, South African, and Western treatments to suit the client's comfort level, values, and worldview. This could involve altering the pace or approach of interventions, integrating family and community assistance where necessary, or fusing evidence-based techniques with culturally based customs. By enabling the treatment process to be responsive rather than prescriptive, flexibility increases participation and the possibility of significant results.

Furthermore, flexibility includes the counsellor's attitude and relationship approach in addition to the approaches they choose. In order to effectively fulfill changing demands, counsellors must constantly monitor and evaluate how clients react to interventions, asking for feedback and making adjustments in real time. It calls for a readiness to combine traditional psychotherapy with non-traditional or culturally unique approaches, as well as an openness to experimentation and creative problem-solving. We can successfully negotiate the challenges of multicultural counselling, forge closer counselling bonds, and deliver interventions that are both clinically and culturally appropriate by developing this flexibility.

Adaptive Use of Counselling Models:

Assessment Phase: Understanding a client's perspective on their problems, what they think would help, and their expectations for counselling all depend on a comprehensive evaluation conducted at the start of treatment. Inquiries such as "What kinds of approaches or traditions do you think might help with challenges like anxiety or depression in your culture?" may be part of this phase, (or worry and sadness keeping in mind that western terms might not be the actual terms used for these issues in their culture).

Integrating Multiple Models: We may blend different counselling approaches based on the needs of the client. A client with depression, for example, can benefit from cognitive behavioural therapy (CBT) to address negative thought patterns and mindfulness exercises based in Daoism to regain emotional equilibrium.

When a client is experiencing bereavement, we may use Ubuntu to highlight the importance of community support, assisting the client in examining their loss within the framework of their social networks and relationships.

Incorporating Chinese Qi Gong or meditation can assist the client manage stress and re-establish a physical, nonverbal connection with themselves, so fostering inner serenity and self-regulation.

Practical Challenges in Adaptability:

Counsellor's Comfort Zone: Counsellors must constantly push themselves out of their own comfort zones. If they are most familiar with Western models (e.g., CBT or psychodynamic therapy), it may feel challenging to integrate South African or Chinese practices, which may be less familiar or more obscure. Overcoming this discomfort and actively learning about new models will expand the counsellor's range and effectiveness.

Client Resistance: Initially, clients may be resistant to new counselling approaches, particularly if they are unfamiliar with models that are not part of their cultural context. For example, the emphasis on community in South African Ubuntu may initially make a customer who strongly connects with Western individualism uneasy. Open communication, concise justifications, and a cooperative approach, however, can lessen resistance.

3. Building Trust and Rapport: The Heart of the Counselling Process

Based on my personal experience, I know that any good counselling relationship is built on rapport and trust. Building a solid relationship with the client based on respect, understanding, and a shared commitment to healing is essential for integrated counseling to be successful. This involves establishing a secure, accepting environment where the client can freely express their feelings, ideas, and cultural convictions. A solid counselling relationship promotes open communication, increases involvement, and enables clients to actively influence the course and emphasis of treatment.

I want to emphasize that trust and rapport are especially crucial in an integrative framework since clients may be juggling several cultural viewpoints at once. It is imperative for us to exhibit cultural humility, carefully listen to our clients' perspectives, and affirm their lived experiences. In addition to more typical counselling procedures, this may entail recognizing the value of spiritual activities, family or community involvement, or traditional healing techniques. Counsellors can improve the efficacy of the counselling process by emphasizing the relational foundation, which encourages collaboration, strengthens the client's sense of agency, and makes sure the integrated approach seems both respectful and personally relevant.

Rapport Building Strategies:

Understanding the Client's Worldview: Establishing a personal connection is only one aspect of developing rapport; another is comprehending and confirming the client's perspective. For instance, familial devotion, or respect for parents and elders, is frequently highly valued in Chinese culture. As a result, the client may consider their family dynamics to be crucial to their counselling process. We can establish rapport and trust with the client by recognizing this cultural value and using it as a starting point.

Cultural Humility: The term "cultural humility" describes a counsellor who is willing to learn from their client rather than only imposing their own cultural viewpoint. For instance, rather than presuming that Western ideas of individualism are universal, a counsellor dealing with South African clients might investigate how Ubuntu—the idea that "I am because we are"—informs the client's sense of self.

Mutual Respect: if a counsellor comes across out as judgmental about cultural customs, beliefs, or life decisions they may lose the client's trust. When working with a Chinese client, for example, a counsellor may need to acknowledge their own prejudices about authoritarian parenting methods and acknowledge that, in Chinese culture, deference to authority and hierarchy is not a negative trait but rather a cultural value.

4. Ethical Considerations in Integrated Counselling: Balancing Traditions and Professional Integrity

If you have been in the academic space long enough, you would know that there are ethical issues to consider with incorporating different therapeutic theories into practice. Counsellors need to be particularly careful to uphold their ethical duties while honoring the cultural customs that their clients bring to the therapy process. In order to keep interventions safe, appropriate, and grounded in evidence, this necessitates giving careful thought to matters like informed consent, confidentiality, boundaries, and professional competence. Counsellors must carefully negotiate cultural practices or beliefs that deviate from accepted counselling norms, striking a balance between their duty to offer ethical and effective care and respect for the client's worldview.

For this integrative approach, ethical practice also involves ongoing monitoring and introspection. I also believe that to prevent forcing our own beliefs on our clients, we need to be aware of their own biases, beliefs, and any blind spots. We should also continue to be open and honest about the reasoning behind each intervention that we have selected, outlining the ways in which various models are being combined. In addition to safeguarding the client's autonomy and right to make knowledgeable decisions about their care, this promotes trust, clarity, and teamwork. We can successfully incorporate several frameworks while making sure that our practice is both responsible and culturally appropriate by retaining ethical vigilance and cultural sensitivity.

Ethical Dilemmas in Integrated Counselling:

Informed Consent and Transparency: When integrating culturally specific models (e.g., traditional South African healing rituals or Chinese spiritual practices like Tai Chi or Qi Gong), the counsellor must make sure that the client fully understands and consents to the methods being employed. This is especially important when introducing spiritual or traditional healing practices that may be unfamiliar or outside the scope of mainstream psychological counselling.

A highly traditionally inclined South African, for instance, would recommend seeing a traditional healer as a component of their treatment. The counsellor must be transparent about the possible advantages and drawbacks of this strategy while maintaining the client's autonomy and right to make an educated decision.

Confidentiality: Maintaining anonymity is another duty of the counsellor, especially when integrating community-based techniques. For example, it's crucial to make clear how information will be exchanged and guarantee that the client's privacy is maintained if the counsellor is working with a community elder.

Navigating Cultural and Professional Boundaries:

Maintaining Professional Boundaries: It is important to maintain the counsellor's professional boundaries even when using conventional therapeutic methods. Even while it could be tempting to work more closely with community healers, the counsellor should always make sure that their approaches are in the best interests of their clients and that they maintain their professional integrity.

Even if a counsellor incorporates community-based healing techniques, they should still lead the therapy process in a way that values the client's independence and promotes their active involvement in choices.

5. Ongoing Professional Development: Evolving as a Culturally Integrated Counsellor

In a society where cultural interactions are becoming more complicated, I would strongly suggest that counsellors need to pursue ongoing professional development to remain effective. This is more than just reading up on the latest research or going to workshops; it's about developing an open-minded and curious mindset regarding the changing global mental health scene. As cultures grow increasingly interconnected, customers may come in with worldviews influenced by a variety of cultural influences, experiences of migration, or traditions passed down through generations. In order to stay updated and productive, counsellors need to make an effort to comprehend these many viewpoints and how they influence their clients' conceptions of healing, suffering, and well-being.

This dedication to development calls for constant introspection and humility. Counsellors must constantly assess how their own cultural experience shapes their perspective and approach to therapy, and they must also be receptive to input from peers and clients.

Professional development, then, I would say is not only about learning new things; but it's also about changing the way counsellors interact with cultural diversity in their work. In order to provide effective interventions, respect the cultural diversity that clients bring to the counselling setting, and adjust their approaches with sensitivity, counsellors must constantly broaden their knowledge and skill set.

Key Development Areas:

Continual Cultural Learning: as counsellors we should always aim to learn more about the customs and cultural backgrounds of the people they are dealing with. This could entail reading up on other therapeutic traditions, obtaining supervision or counsel from other practitioners, or participating in cultural competence training.

Seeking Supervision: When dealing with different models, counsellors may encounter difficulties, particularly when cultural quirks clash with conventional counselling methods. The counsellor can manage moral quandaries or emotional tiredness while remaining culturally sensitive to the client's requirements with the support of regular supervision and peer consultation, which can offer the insight and direction that is required.

Self-Reflection: Counsellors who want to integrate culturally must constantly reflect on their own prejudices, cultural presumptions, and emotional reactions to their clients. They can stay effective, kind, and morally rooted in their profession by engaging in this introspective practice.

Conclusion: Embracing Complexity in Integrated Counselling

In integrated counselling, the counsellor plays a difficult yet incredibly fulfilling function. In its place, it urges practitioners to embrace cultural humility, adaptability, and a continuous dedication to moral behavior and lifelong learning. Through the integration of Western psychology, South African Ubuntu philosophy, and Chinese ideas of harmony and balance, counsellors may provide clients with a comprehensive counselling framework that values both individual development and group well-being. In addition to managing their challenges, this integration enables clients to discover purpose, resiliency, and strength in ways that are culturally authentic, spiritually meaningful, and personal.

Look, we are in an age of mental health care that embraces diversity as a source of creativity and strength rather than a hindrance and this is all thanks to integrated counseling. Although the focus of this book has been on Chinese, South African, and Western customs, the vision is far broader. In addition to learning from their clients' customs and practices, I stand on the fact that it pushes counsellors worldwide to maintain their curiosity and view every counselling interaction as a cross-cultural exchange of knowledge. In this way, as counselors we can contribute to the development of a worldwide counselling profession that is dynamic, inclusive, and sensitive to the needs of a globalized society. The ability to adapt, respect cultural diversity, and establish environments where each client feels seen, understood, and supported on their path to recovery and wholeness is ultimately what will determine the future of counselling.

Chapter 7

Future Directions in Integrated Counselling

In my opinion, without suggesting the decolonization of psychology, psychological counseling techniques must change to accommodate clients from a broad range of cultural, social, and spiritual backgrounds as the globe grows more linked and diverse. Counsellors now deal with clients whose views, values, and coping mechanisms are influenced by a variety of cultural factors; they are no longer working with homogeneous populations. Counselling must therefore change to include adaptability, cultural sensitivity, and an openness to different philosophies.

An important and essential stage in this progress is the integrating of Chinese, South African, and Western approaches and models. Western methods contribute research-informed tactics, systematic treatments, and evidence-based frameworks. With an emphasis on spirituality, social connectivity, and community resilience, South African viewpoints provide communal, relational, and contextual understandings of mental health. Chinese approaches, which have their roots in holistic perspectives on the mind and body, place a strong emphasis on harmony, balance, and the interaction of physical, emotional, and spiritual well-being. When combined, these systems provide a deeper, more complex counselling basis that enables counsellors to customize interventions to each client's particular cultural and personal circumstances.

My view is that this integration is just the start, though. Counselling will require even more flexibility in the future as cultures grow more interconnected and clients' experiences cross cultural barriers more frequently. Counsellors will need to expand their cultural competency into new settings and modalities in response to emerging trends, such as the increasing use of digital platforms, teletherapy, and virtual support networks. Research on post-traumatic growth, trauma-informed treatment, and culturally entrenched coping mechanisms will also continue to influence evidence-based approaches, providing counsellors with increasingly advanced resources to help clients in a variety of settings.

My two cents is that the function of the counsellor is essential to this development. Future practitioners will need to develop a lifelong commitment to learning, ethical flexibility, and a profound cultural humility in addition to their theoretical and technical proficiency. They must develop into adept multi-framework navigators who can incorporate elements of Chinese, South African, Western, and other cultural viewpoints while maintaining the integrity of each system. In the end, integrated counseling's future lies not just in merging approaches but in developing a dynamic, adaptable, and culturally sensitive practice that enables clients to recover in ways that have great personal significance.

1. The Globalization of Counselling Practices: Expanding the Scope of Integration

In this changing environment, integrated counselling will need to do much more than just combine Chinese, South African, and Western models. I would like to think that practice will necessitate an even more comprehensive toolset that incorporates a wide variety of cultural viewpoints and healing methods from around the world, even if these three frameworks offer a solid foundation. Indigenous methods from the Americas, African ideologies outside of South Africa, South Asian and Middle Eastern frameworks, and contemporary hybrid cultural identities influenced by digital globalization are a few examples of this.

This kind of expansion of the counselling toolkit entails developing a greater level of cultural literacy and humility rather than merely adopting methods or converting behaviors into a psychological framework. Counsellors must comprehend the lived relevance, social implications, and ethical bounds of various cultural models in addition to their theoretical foundations. By doing this, they can interact with clients in ways that are genuine and appropriate for the situation, enabling interventions that respect the clients' experiences, values, and beliefs.

Ultimately, as society becomes more globalized, counselling has the chance to develop into a really multicultural and culturally sensitive profession that can assist clients whose experiences cut across social, cultural, and geographic boundaries. Therefore, the future of integrated counselling is not just about bridging current paradigms but also about developing a broad, flexible, and morally sound framework that can adapt to our increasingly diverse and linked world.

Key Trends in Globalization and Counselling:

Transnational Counselling: Counsellors will need to comprehend how diverse cultural traditions influence mental health and recovery across continents as more individuals live and work internationally. For instance, as counsellors we will need to become knowledgeable about and incorporate the unique cultural beliefs and customs of the expanding African, South Asian, and Latin American movements.

Culturally Relevant Models: A greater range of cultural approaches will be introduced into the counselling setting in the future of integrated counseling. There may be even more culturally sensitive approaches to treating trauma, anxiety, and depression if South Asian spiritual practices, African Indigenous healing practices, and Latin American counselling paradigms are combined.

Global Mental Health Networks: Global mental health networks will be facilitated by the growing connectedness through digital platforms, allowing clients and counselors from other nations to exchange ideas, methods, and practices. A broader and more varied body of counselling knowledge will result from these global interactions.

2. Technology and Counselling: Digital Platforms and Cross-Cultural Integration

Technology's quick development will keep changing how counsellors combine various counselling models, especially in cross-cultural settings. AI-assisted interventions, online counseling services, and teletherapy are not just convenient tools; they are radically changing how therapy is provided, accessed, and experienced. I mean we are already counselling online. It was formerly challenging to give culturally specific counselling, but now clients from a variety of cultural backgrounds can interact with counsellors across geographic boundaries.

Additionally, technology offers chances to more methodically integrate cultural aspects into counseling. Digital platforms, for example, can provide culturally appropriate psychoeducation, resources in many languages, and interactive technologies that represent the values, belief systems, and communication styles of their clients. By offering real-time reminders to take cultural context into account while developing interventions, AI-assisted systems may help counsellors identify culturally impacted thought or behavior patterns. These technologies can improve a counsellor's ability to address each client's particular cultural demands, but they cannot replace professional judgment or human empathy.

I think we must be cognizant of the fact that these developments also bring with them new difficulties. Digital accessibility, data privacy, and the danger of reducing culturally rich experiences to standardized algorithms are all challenges that counsellors must deal with. Furthermore, because teletherapy is remote, it may be more challenging to notice nonverbal clues, relational dynamics, or subtle cultural cues—all of which are crucial in cross-cultural counselling.

Technology finally has the ability to increase integrated counselling's reach, adaptability, and cultural responsiveness in spite of these obstacles. Counsellors can develop evidence-based and culturally sensitive interventions by carefully fusing digital tools with conventional therapeutic models. This helps to close gaps between Western, South African, Chinese, and other cultural approaches. As a result, technology is no longer merely a means of delivery but also a tool for improving the breadth, accessibility, and applicability of counseling in a society growing more interconnected by the day.

Technology's Role in Expanding Cultural Integration:

Virtual counselling: With the growing popularity of virtual counseling, counsellors can now deal with clients from a variety of cultural backgrounds, particularly those who might not otherwise have access to mental health care in their area. Counselors will be able to offer culturally sensitive interventions through digital platforms without being restricted by regional boundaries. For clients in underserved or remote areas where access to standard mental health care may be limited, this is especially important.

Digital Cultural Competence Tools: New digital technologies that help therapists better understand how a client's culture shapes their worldview include machine learning-based speech pattern analysis, AI-guided counselling frameworks, and cultural competency tests. These resources can provide suggestions for culturally appropriate modifications to standard counselling techniques, enabling real-time practice customization for counsellors.

Online Communities and Shared Knowledge: Counsellors from various cultural backgrounds will be able to exchange experiences and methods through online communities and networks such as forums, webinars, and virtual conferences. Practitioners will be able to share information about particular cultural models and integrated counseling best practices in these areas.

3. Interdisciplinary Collaborations: Blending Psychology with Other Fields

On a much broader perspective I suggest we ponder on how collaboration between psychology and complementary disciplines including anthropology, sociology, spiritual studies, and medicine will become more and more important for integrated counselling in the future. Every one of these fields offers distinct perspectives that enhance the counselling procedure. For example, sociology and anthropology provide frameworks for comprehending the social structures, cultural norms, and community dynamics of the client, which might influence their resilience, coping, and stress experiences. Spiritual studies help counsellors navigate their clients' spiritual or religious frameworks with competence and respect by offering information on the significance of belief systems, rituals, and existential meaning in mental health.

I would like to highlight that by providing counsellors with knowledge on the biological and physiological foundations of mental health, medicine— and psychosomatic research—ensures that interventions are comprehensive and based on a knowledge of the mind and body. Counsellors are able to develop more comprehensive, contextually aware treatment programs that take into account all of the variables affecting a client's well-being by utilizing these several fields.

Additionally, the development of these counselling techniques is fostered by interdisciplinary collaboration. To integrate mental health assistance into primary healthcare, for instance, counsellors can collaborate with medical experts. They might also collaborate with cultural anthropologists to create community-based interventions that respect regional customs and values. To jointly develop culturally aware programs that connect psychological theory with lived experience, spiritual counselors and community leaders can be enlisted. In addition to improving the efficacy of counseling interventions, these partnerships deepen the therapist's comprehension of the human condition and promote flexibility, humility, and lifelong learning. Counseling eventually develops into a genuinely comprehensive, client-centered approach that is sensitive to the complicated reality of many populations thanks to the integration of insights from several disciplines. These are all just far away thoughts, just for discussion purposes.

Potential Interdisciplinary Collaborations:

Anthropology and Psychology: Anthropology provides important insights into social structures, rituals, and cultural ideas. Counsellors can gain a deeper understanding of the cultural frameworks that influence a client's identity, worldview, and coping strategies by working with anthropologists. Counsellors can better integrate cultural healing methods and negotiate difficult cultural issues with the support of this relationship.

Spirituality and Counselling: Many clients may place a high value on spirituality and religious practices in relation to their mental health, particularly those from Asian and African cultures. More partnerships between counsellors and clergy or spiritual leaders may be common in the future of integrated counseling, providing a more comprehensive therapeutic approach that takes into account the spiritual aspects of the human condition.

Collaborating with Traditional Healers: Traditional healers are essential to the mental health of the population in South Africa and many other Asian countries. In order to connect contemporary counselling techniques with conventional healing systems, integrated counseling will probably include closer cooperation with these healers. Co-facilitated sessions, collaborative consultations, or counselling workshops that blend conventional and scientific approaches are a few examples of this.

4. Training the Next Generation of Culturally Competent Counsellors

In my opinion, the future generation of counsellors must have the abilities, know-how, and open-mindedness to interact politely and productively with various cultural traditions in order to properly integrate varied counselling approaches. This encompasses a thorough awareness of the social circumstances, communication styles, cultural norms, and belief systems that affect mental health in addition to technical competence in counseling procedures. Since clients may rely on customs, worldviews, and coping mechanisms that diverge greatly from Western psychological frameworks, counsellors must also develop empathy, adaptability, and humility. By strengthening these skills, therapists can modify interventions in ways that are morally and culturally appropriate, making therapy relevant and successful for clients from a variety of backgrounds.

In light of all this, I personally suggest that the training of counselors must be significantly altered in order to reach this level of cultural competency. To properly integrate cultural literacy into every facet of the curriculum, from fundamental theory to the development of practical skills, academic programs must go beyond tokenistic cultural awareness courses. Clinical training should involve exposure to non-Western therapeutic modalities, opportunities to work with community leaders or traditional healers, and supervised interactions with clients from a variety of ethnic backgrounds. Furthermore, cultivating the self-awareness and flexibility required for integrated counseling requires reflective practices, mentorship, and continual professional development. The sector may teach therapists who are not only technically skilled but also competent to handle the complexity of a multicultural, international clientele by rethinking training in this way.

Cultural Immersion Programs: In the future, counseling programs might incorporate cultural involvement experiences, in which students work in cross-cultural environments both domestically and overseas. Counsellors will have the opportunity to see firsthand the dynamics of many cultures through these programs, and they will learn how to incorporate these experiences into their counselling work.

Cross-Cultural Supervision: Cross-cultural mentorship, in which experienced counsellors offer advice on incorporating culturally varied models into practice, will become a part of supervision models in the future. Case studies, peer-reviewed cultural evaluations, and conversations about moral conundrums that come up while working with clients from different cultural backgrounds are a few examples of this.

Incorporating Indigenous Healing Methods into Training: Traditional counselling paradigms and Indigenous healing practices may become more and more integrated into the curricula of counselling programs. Training facilities will equip aspiring counsellors to provide genuinely integrated treatment by acknowledging these techniques as legitimate and useful instruments in contemporary counselling.

5. Expanding the Definition of Mental Health and Wellness

Generally, I would say that beyond the conventional emphasis on symptom relief or personal psychological functioning, the notion of mental health itself is anticipated to broaden as integrated counselling gains traction. I further believe that a wider, more comprehensive view of well-being will be embraced by future viewpoints, acknowledging the close connections between mental health and its physical, emotional, social, and spiritual aspects. This method accepts that the mind and body are intertwined and that emotional anguish frequently shows up as physical symptoms, problems in relationships, or disturbances in one's sense of meaning and purpose.

This holistic approach also acknowledges that healing is a societal and cultural process rather than just an individual one. Spiritual or religious views, cultural customs, familial relationships, and community support all have an impact on well-being. For example, counselling sessions may combine evidence-based counselling techniques with culturally appropriate coping strategies, family participation, or community rituals. A more complex view of what it means to be resilient, healthy, and fulfilled is fostered by integrated counseling, which places mental health within these larger settings. By doing this, the discipline advances toward a care paradigm that respects the entire diversity of the human experience and unites scientific understanding with spiritual and cultural wisdom to promote recovery that is truly sustainable.

Redefining Mental Health:

Holistic Health Models: Holistic approaches that emphasize the harmony of mind, body, and spirit will be the norm in mental health treatment in the future. Ideally, I think counsellors will receive training on how to evaluate mental health using various perspectives, emphasizing the value of family, community, spirituality, and individual identity.

Collective Well-being: The concept of community well-being will become more prevalent in counselling settings as a result of inspiration from African philosophies like Ubuntu and communal healing techniques. I also think that interventions in mental health will increasingly acknowledge that community support is just as important to healing as individual healing.

Culturally Informed Frameworks: Counselling models will become more culturally sensitive. Counselling will be viewed as a dynamic, relational, and collaborative process rather than as a Western, individualistic endeavor. Recognizing the distinct ways that other cultures define and approach well-being, therapists will integrate cultural practices and beliefs into their counselling strategies.

6. Overcoming Challenges and Embracing Opportunities in Integrated Counselling

Even if there is a lot of room for improvement, I still stand on the fact that a few major obstacles need to be overcome before integrated counselling can reach its full potential. Managing cultural variations without simplifying or stealing varied methods is one of the main issues. The significance and efficacy of rich cultural or spiritual traditions could be diminished if counsellors were to convert them to merely methods or instruments within a Western psychological paradigm. Furthermore, it is crucial to uphold the ethical and professional bounds of counselling, making sure that therapists respect their clients' cultural and spiritual demands while avoiding taking on tasks or obligations outside of their training.

With all this being said, when I look at the whole integration approach, I still think that counselor preparation and training present another significant obstacle. In addition to technical expertise, deep cultural literacy, self-awareness, and continuous reflective practice are necessary for integrating many counselling methods. Curricula that offer possibilities for multidisciplinary collaboration, supervised practical experience with culturally diverse clientele, and meaningful exposure to diverse frameworks must be developed by educational institutions and professional bodies. It is also necessary to address institutional and logistical obstacles, such as equitable service distribution, resources for continuing professional development, and access to culturally competent supervision.

Lastly, I highlight that as globalization and technology continue to change clientele and delivery methods, counselors need to be flexible and receptive to new ideas while cautiously addressing concerns about privacy, accessibility, and cultural sensitivity. The full potential of integrated counselling as a comprehensive, culturally sensitive, and successful method of mental health treatment can only be realized by directly addressing these issues.

Challenges to Anticipate:

Cultural Misunderstandings: counsellors who work with clients from different cultural backgrounds may run into miscommunications or resistance from others in the field. Conflicts between the client's cultural expectations and the counsellor's theoretical stance may occur.

Ethical Dilemmas: There are ethical questions regarding professional boundaries, cultural appropriateness, and the possibility of injury when contemporary psychological techniques are used with traditional methods. It will be necessary for counsellors to create explicit rules for handling these moral dilemmas.

Training and Resources: Barriers may arise from counsellors not having enough resources to participate in cross-cultural training. To guarantee that counsellors can satisfy the rising demand for integrated counseling services, professional development in this area will be essential.

Opportunities Ahead:

A New Paradigm for counselling: Counsellors will have the chance to participate in a changing counselling paradigm that is more inclusive, flexible, and holistic as more patients seek out culturally relevant care. This makes it possible for counseling methods to become more inventive, creative, and successful.

Healing Beyond Borders: As more patients look for culturally appropriate care, counsellors will have the opportunity to be part of a shifting counselling paradigm that is more flexible, inclusive, and holistic. This enables counselling approaches to become more successful, innovative, and creative.

Conclusion: Paving the Way for Future Counselling Practices

In light of all this, I would like to highlight in this conclusion that integrated counselling has a bright future filled with expansion, promise, and deep cultural appreciation. Counsellors will come across clients whose identities, values, and coping mechanisms straddle several cultural contexts as global migration picks up speed and cultural barriers become more pliable. The way counselling is provided is being further transformed by technological developments such as teletherapy, online platforms, and AI-assisted technologies, which open up new ways to connect with clients across geographical and cultural barriers. As counsellors we need to learn how to handle intricate cultural variables in this changing environment to make sure their interventions are morally righteous and culturally relevant.

Further, as counsellors we can provide complete and culturally relevant counselling by incorporating Western, South African, Chinese, and other cultural frameworks. Based on what I discussed across the book, Chinese techniques prioritize balance, harmony, and overall well-being, South African viewpoints stress relational and communal resilience, while Western approaches offer structured, evidence-based ways. When combined, these frameworks offer a multifaceted counselling foundation that enables professionals to customize interventions that target the social, emotional, physical, and spiritual aspects of each client's experience. Through this I believe counsellors can respect their clients' worldviews without appropriating or oversimplifying them by adopting a variety of frameworks, which promotes counselling efficacy and trust.

Additionally, and as I said, maybe not in the near future but in many years to come, a dedication to interdisciplinary collaboration is necessary for the future of counselling. Important insights into the cultural, social, and biological elements that influence mental health can be gained from disciplines like anthropology, sociology, spiritual studies, and medicine. As counsellors we can create counselling sessions that are not only mentally sound but also contextually and culturally aware by collaborating across disciplines. Innovative treatment methods, community-based initiatives, and holistic approaches that acknowledge the interdependence of social, cultural, and individual well-being are encouraged by this cooperative approach. Additionally, it improves the counsellor's ability to think critically, practice reflectively, and be flexible skills that will be crucial in a clientele that is increasingly globalized and culturally varied.

Lastly, I believe that ability to accept variety, promote cross-cultural interactions, and develop strong interpersonal and community ties is ultimately what will determine the future of integrated counselling. The collaborative nature of healing is becoming more widely acknowledged, encompassing not only the person but also families, communities, and cultural customs. To promote holistic well-being, as counsellors, we will need to cultivate cultural humility, broaden their understanding of many healing traditions, and make use of emerging technologies. Within the vastness of human experience, integrated counselling can develop into a practice that enables clients to navigate complexity, develop resilience, and experience meaningful progress by combining evidence-based methods, culturally grounded practices, and community knowledge.

Epilogue: The Path Forward: Healing in the Global Age

As I reach the end of this exploration into the integration of Western, South African, and Chinese counselling methodologies, one thing has become clear to me is that the future of counselling is really about cultural understanding and integration as it is about the science of counselling itself.

I recognize that in the coming decades, the world will continue to change—cultural boundaries will blur, migration patterns will shift, and diverse identities will increasingly intersect. My ability to adapt, to learn from, and to integrate various cultural models will define the quality and relevance of the care I offer. This book, therefore, is not just an end but the beginning of an ongoing journey—one that calls on me to remain open to the richness of different healing practices, to continue expanding my cultural competence, and to engage with clients in ways that honour their unique identities and histories.

For me, the integration of Western, South African, and Chinese models reflects the globalized world in which I practice. It is a call to embrace the diversity of human experience and to weave that richness into the fabric of my counselling work. I believe the future of counselling lies not in isolating counselling models into silos, but in bringing them together, allowing me to craft interventions that are as diverse and complex as the individuals I serve.

Ultimately, my goal as a mental health professional is to provide healing that transcends cultural boundaries, recognizing the universal needs of the human condition while also respecting the specific cultural influences that shape each individual. In this way, counselling becomes a shared, global journey that connects us all in our pursuit of well-being. As I move forward in my practice, I am reminded that integrated counselling is not a destination but a continuous process of growth, reflection, and adaptation. By approaching every client through the lens of cultural sensitivity, empathy, and respect, I can enhance their healing journey while deepening my own understanding of what it truly means to be a culturally competent counsellor.

Note to Readers: While this book is written from my personal journey and perspective, the ideas are informed by many scholars, practitioners, and traditions. The following references guided my thinking and may serve as resources for those who want to explore these themes more deeply.

Reference List

1. American Psychological Association. (2017). *Multicultural guidelines: An ecological approach to context, identity, and intersectionality*. American Psychological Association.
2. Bojuwoye, O. (2005). Traditional healing practices in Southern Africa: An examination of the role of traditional healers. *Indilinga: African Journal of Indigenous Knowledge Systems, 4*(1), 57–69.
3. Eagle, G., & Kaminer, D. (2013). Continuous traumatic stress: Expanding the lexicon of traumatic stress. *Peace and Conflict: Journal of Peace Psychology, 19*(2), 85–99.
4. Edwards, D. (2005). *Critical issues in clinical and health psychology*. Cape Town: UCT Press.
5. Freud, S. (1917). *Introductory lectures on psycho-analysis*. New York: Liveright.
6. Janzen, J. M. (1992). *Ngoma: Discourses of healing in Central and Southern Africa*. Berkeley: University of California Press.

7. Kaptchuk, T. J. (2000). *The web that has no weaver: Understanding Chinese medicine*. Chicago, IL: McGraw-Hill.
8. Kleinman, A. (1980). *Patients and healers in the context of culture: An exploration of the borderland between anthropology, medicine, and psychiatry*. Berkeley: University of California Press.
9. Laungani, P. (2004). *Asian perspectives in counselling and psychotherapy*. London: Routledge.
10. Marsella, A. J., & Yamada, A. M. (2010). Culture and psychopathology: Foundations, issues, directions. *Journal of Pacific Rim Psychology, 4*(2), 103–115.
11. Moodley, R., & Palmer, S. (Eds.). (2006). *Race, culture and psychotherapy: Critical perspectives in multicultural practice*. London: Routledge.
12. Moodley, R., & West, W. (Eds.). (2005). *Integrating traditional healing practices into counselling and psychotherapy*. Thousand Oaks, CA: Sage.
13. Peltzer, K. (2009). Traditional health practitioners in South Africa. *The Lancet, 374*(9694), 956–957.
14. Rogers, C. R. (1961). *On becoming a person: A therapist's view of psychotherapy*. Boston: Houghton Mifflin.
15. Seedat, M., Duncan, N., & Lazarus, S. (2001). *Community psychology: Theory, method, and practice in South Africa*. Cape Town: Oxford University Press.

16. Sue, D. W., & Sue, D. (2016). *Counseling the culturally diverse: Theory and practice* (7th ed.). Hoboken, NJ: Wiley.
17. Tao, J. (2013). Traditional Chinese philosophy and psychotherapy. *Journal of Chinese Philosophy, 40*(3–4), 439–456.
18. Thompson, C. E., & McRae, M. B. (2001). *Counseling ethnic minorities: Theory and practice* (2nd ed.). New York: McGraw-Hill.
19. Tseng, W. (2001). *Handbook of cultural psychiatry*. San Diego: Academic Press.
20. Watters, E. (2010). *Crazy like us: The globalization of the American psyche*. New York: Free Press.